The Illusion of Competence:

An Innovative Leader's Guide to

Innovative Leadership

Mark Branson

The Illusion of Competence:

An Innovative Leader's Guide to

Innovative Leadership

Mark Branson

Preface

Winning the Conflict between Middle and Upper Management

Top Executives at large corporations are responsible for determining the direction of companies. Upper Management develops strategies, provides guidance, and issues instructions to achieve predetermined directives. Upper management uses multiple methods to guide the direction of corporations. Business management books offer executives guidance on how to run companies. Executives across various fields use similar methods to run companies based on the philosophies in widely read business leadership books.

Corporations rely on middle managers to carry out directives. Commands are then handed down by top level executives. Due to the proximity to the front lines, middle managers have the insight, skills, and ability to develop and implement strategies that associates will be excited to execute, without reading outdated leadership books with questionable philosophies.

The Nature of the Conflict

Thirty years of experience in retail management has led to an awareness of conflict that exists between middle and upper management. Upper level executives send down directives that middle managers are expected to implement with subordinates; however, experience indicates that the buy-in of lower level associates is limited. Upper management goes as far as to threaten the employment of mid-level managers and lower level associates if directives are not followed to a tee. Having witnessed a lack of support for directives by upper management across several companies, the thought occurred that maybe the problem was not a result of insubordination among employees. Is there a possibility that the concepts from above are out of touch with the realities of day to day operations? The contention is that executives are ill-equipped to provide meaningful directions due to the separation and lack of respect for day-to-day operations. Middle management is better qualified to identify and implement the programs that will lead companies to succeed because mid-level managers gain first-hand knowledge of the programs and the response from employees and customers.

Upper management and strategizing

In general, upper management is not overly concerned with middle management's attitudes and emotions. Instead, executives focus solely on task completion, even when encountering repeated pushback from middle management during implementation. Scholars of strategy implementation have been inclined to adopt an "affect neutral" viewpoint that concentrates on bounded rationality, reasoning, and task-related measurements. For example, executing a new strategy can be more successful when top executives express the vision plainly and design applicable task systems including formal structures, control systems, and enticements. New strategy and the logic of comparison among numerous task systems are expected to align performance at various levels of the organization. Additionally, scholars that have embraced a cognitive focus have explores ways company employees make sense of strategic actions and how employee analysis influences later decisions (Huy, 2011).

These research viewpoints, although intuitive, have overlooked how the emotions of middle managers impact policy acceptance. Since middle managers occupy leadership positions, middle managers' emotions can influence how subordinates think and behave (Sy, Cˆot´e, and Saavedra, 2005). For these reasons, top-level executives should pay closer attention when middle managers are not supportive of directives.

Influential Business Management Books

"Who Moved My Cheese", one of the 25 highest rated business management books of all time according to Time magazine, has sold 20 million copies (Sachs, 2009). The author, Spencer Johnson, co-authored another book on the top 25 list with Kenneth Blanchard, "The One Minute Manager". Additionally, Blanchard is often credited with the founding of the SMART goal acronym (Morrison, 2010), though research indicates otherwise.

Business leadership books are big business. Blanchard, a man of faith, goes by the self-glossed title of Chief Spiritual Officer at the Blanchard Training and Development firm. Blanchard has parleyed The One Minute Manager into speaking engagements, up to 100 per year, during the past 20 years. The current fee to listen to Blanchard is $50,000 per lecture, which would put the gross aggregate fees, in 2001 dollars, at roughly $100 million (Teresi, 2001).

"Who Moved My Cheese" spent over ten years on the "New York Times" best seller list, but prior to meeting Blanchard at a dinner party in 1980, Johnson was best known as a veteran writer of children's' books. In fact, Johnson was working on a booked titled "The One Minute Parent" when Blanchard recommended the two join forces to write a leadership book (Teresi, 2001). Johnson's background in children's books might explain why both the One Minute Manager and Who Moved My Cheese are such easy reads.

Lastly, Blanchard faced charges of plagiarism from a colleague Blanchard worked with in 1976. Elliott Carlisle, a business instructor at the University of Massachusetts at Amherst, put out "MacGregor," a piece written in an avant-garde parable form, in the Organizational Dynamics Journal. When placed side by side, The One Minute Manager is a carbon copy of the article for the first 49 pages. Interestingly, Blanchard does not deny borrowing heavily from the Carlisle's article. Instead, Blanchard claims that contributions to MacGregor justified the use of the article's content and denied plagiarism occurred in writing The One Minute Manager (Teresi, 2001).

The One Minute Manager

The One Minute Manager divulges three secrets to creative and capable managing as detailed through the search for the perfect managing and leading principles. The One Minute Manager is fixated on the three secrets of success used by a leader that has earned the respect of fellow employees. The secrets of the one minute manager include setting one minute goals, offering one minute praises to employees, and lastly, giving employees one minute reprimands (Spamer, n.d.).

The short book, often criticized as simple-minded, spent two years on The New York Times best seller list. Interestingly, the authors were accused of plagiarism by the Wall Street Journal, a charge the authors denied. Carlisle claims MacGregor is his creation. Carlisle characterizes the co-authorship claim as absurd (Teresi, 2001). By the time the Wall Street Journal had made the accusation, the little volume was omnipresent, having been distributed by Fortune 500 companies around the country (Sachs, 2011).

The Seven Habits of Highly Effective People

"The Seven Habits of Highly Effective People" was written by Stephen Covey and first published in 1989. Though highly educated, Covey makes no claim that the seven habits are original thoughts. In fact, Covey claims that the seven habits are sprinkled throughout religions around the world, 'self-evident', and above reproach. If there is a sense of religious overtone to the seven habits, look no further than Brigham Young University, the university Covey spent the bulk of his career as a professor teaching organizational behavior and business management (White Dove, n.d.).

According to Gandel (2011), "The fact that the seven "habits" overlap and aren't all that revelatory — No. 2 boils down to focusing on your goals — hasn't seemed to blunt the book's continuing popularity".

Who Moved My Cheese?

The premise behind Who Moved My Cheese is simple. Change is inevitable and should be embraced. The book has a cult following, including top CEOs, which claim the book has been life and work altering. The book has been distributed by business leaders far and wide, with the goal of decreasing employee resistance to change. Though "Who Moved My Cheese" has been hit with parodies by detractors, the book still managed to be the best-selling business book in history with over 20 million copies sold around the world (Sachs, 2011).

After reading Who Moved My Cheese, an interesting fact came to light. The book makes no attempt to validate the need for change, only that change is inevitable. The book invites people to accept change without question. Conveniently, the people that benefit the most from blindly accepting change are the executives issuing directives employees do not like, yet Johnson would have people believe questioning change is a problem to be overcome.

Turns out, Who Moved My Cheese is used by executives to lower resistance to new programs. Executives do not have to be held accountable for bad ideas if there is no challenging of the process. Middle management has the ability and knowledge to analyze the effectiveness of new programs. Who Moved My Cheese would have readers believe the services of middle management are not needed to scrutinize the decisions from above.

There are several interesting parallels among The One Minute Manager, 7 Habits of Highly Effective People, and Who Moved My Cheese. The three books lack ground breaking ideas, have sold millions of copies, have been widely read by business leaders, and the leaders have used the books to guide middle management and associates. As a result, the popularity of business leadership books of suspect quality lends credence to the idea that middle management benefits from not knowing information widely circulated among upper management.

Popular Business Acronyms

Business acronyms are used as tools to present ideas to associates in a manner that is easy to remember. Companies also incorporate outside concepts into everyday operations through the use of acronyms. Problems arise when acronyms appear trite or fail to deliver on the promise to improve operations.

SMART Goals

SMART goals are specific, measurable, attainable, realistic, and tangible. The interesting thing about SMART goals is that the origin of the acronym is difficult to ascertain. The term has been attributed to authors that referenced SMART goals in different generations. Common credit was given to Peter Drucker in the 1954 book "The Practice of Management"; however, closer inspection revealed the term was never used in the book. Kenneth Blanchard referenced SMART goals in the book, "Leadership and the One Minute Manager" in 1985, with the only difference being that the "T" stands for "Trackable" instead of "Tangible". Blanchard again referenced the acronym when writing "Management of Organizational Behavior" with Paul Hersey in 1988. Even though SMART goals were clearly stated in the 1988 book, a claim exists that Paul Meyer first used the term in 1965 in the book, "Personal Success Planner". The interesting thing about Meyer is that he developed SMART goals to influence his personal actions with his child, not the actions of those around him (Morrison, 2010).

SMARTER goals

SMARTER goals add two additional letters to the existing acronym. The "E" stands for "Evaluate" while the "R" means "Re-Do". The meaning of "Evaluate" is to analyze the effectiveness of the SMART process, while "Re-Do" means to restart the SMARTER process after completing the evaluation (S.M.A.R.T.E.R. Goals, n.d.). The fact that SMART goals led to smarter goals indicates the shortcomings of both acronyms.

SERVE

The SERVE selling model is used by Visionworks to guide associates in offering assistance to customers. SERVE stands for "Smile and Greet", "Explore Needs", "Reflect and Listen", "Voice Recommendations", and "End by Close". The idea behind SERVE is to have a uniform selling model used by employees throughout the 700 North American stores. Though the stated goal is to provide the best possible service, the true purpose is to identify opportunities to sell upgraded frame and lens options to customers.

Business Acronym Shortcomings

Having worked for Visionworks for two years as a mid-level store manager and for three years as a general manager for Lenscrafters, a company that used a selling model similar to SERVE, there was first-hand knowledge of the lack of support for 'acronym' based selling models at the middle management and associate level of the corporate hierarchy. The feedback from employees was the SERVE selling model resulted in rigid customer interactions that lacked personality on the part of associates. Tellingly, upper management attempted to train employees to present SERVE in a natural and comfortable manner, even though the goal was for employees to act in a uniform fashion.

As a manager, SERVE was recognized as useful in new associate training for providing employees with a solid sales foundation until the understanding of the complex eyewear business had improved; however, the SERVE selling model was of little value for experienced employees because building quality relationships with consumers was muted when employee interactions appeared unnatural. The pushback from employees in regards to SERVE was pronounced, especially considering employees earned attractive sales commissions. The thought that employees were unreceptive to a program designed to increase commissions made little sense. The obvious reason employees did not embrace SERVE was because the program did not work.

Interestingly, SMART goals have a large following in the upper levels of the business world even though the term's origin is surrounded by ambiguity. To further muddy the waters, an author recognized with inventing SMART goals had previously been accused of plagiarism, raising additional questions about SMART goals' credibility.

Struggling Corporations and Business Philosophies

Large Corporations come and go on a regular basis. Examples of recently failed companies include Montgomery Wards, Circuit City, Enron, World Com, among many others. Businesses on the current watch list include Sears, Best Buy, and JC Penney. Businesses, successes or failures, have at least one common denominator. Businesses follow specific operational theories that dictates day-to-day operations.

Six Sigma

Six Sigma is a quality improvement program created by Motorola in the 1980s. Variations of Six Sigma like "Design for Six Sigma", "Lean Six Sigma", and problem-solving applications used in the manufacturing and service sectors, have continued to appeal to the global community. However, detractors have questioned Six Sigma efficacy claims made by supporters, and academic organizations commonly do not view Six Sigma as a prescription for excellence (Goh, 2012).

Home Depot

Home Depot adopted Six Sigma in 2001 after hiring Robert Nardelli as Chief Executive Officer. Nardelli was a Six Sigma disciple, having worked as an executive for General Electric, an early convert to the quality improvement process. Though factors like a terse management style and a large compensation package contributed to Nardelli's demise, Home Depot stock price languished under Six Sigma dogma during the S&P 500 and housing boon of the early 2000s (Richardson, 2007).

Toyota Production System

The Toyota 'lean' manufacturing system and culture of constant enhancement were the envy of the business community (Wu, Blos, Wee, & Chen, 2010). An essential belief of the Toyota Production System was that the company paid attention to the 'voice of the customer' and delivered features and functions in vehicles that, at the least, met customer requirements. Toyota owners wanted safety, but safety standards had not been met (Mojonnier, 2010).

Toyota

Toyota has often been viewed as the apex of Japanese innovation, industrial quality and manufacturing strength, especially after overtaking General Motors in 2008 and becoming the largest automotive manufacturer on the planet (Wu, Blos, Wee, & Chen, 2010), but the accolades that came with becoming number one were short-lived. Toyota faced numerous challenges within the corporate culture and automobile market environment. The company, famous for quality, had to rebuild a reputation built on lean production and safety (Taneja, Pryor, and Sewell, 2012).

Servant Leadership

Robert Greenleaf founded servant leadership after reading "Journey to the East" by Hermann Hesse. The premise was that the leader becomes a leader through the service and prioritizing of the needs of others. Servant Leadership also relies heavily on the teachings of Jesus Christ and the Bible (Greenleaf, 2016).

The primary issue with servant leadership is that the concept is presented as a "can't miss" leadership philosophy. As a consequence, servant leadership companies that struggle draw the validity of the philosophy into question. The number of companies that claim to be servant leadership companies also raises questions about the nature of the philosophy. For example, Southwest Airlines, Starbucks, and Chick-Fil-A are some known servant leadership standard bearers, but companies like Walmart and 7-11 also have claimed servant leadership status (Modern Servant, 2016). Walmart faces millions in litigation annually to resolve employee labor issues while convenience stores are known for high turnover, low morale, and dangerous work environments, none of which are considered servant leadership strengths.

Lower management and implementation.

According to recent studies, there are three views on the role of middle management in strategy implementation. The first view is that middle managers are implementers of policies advanced by top-management teams. This traditional view holds that middle managers are the 'linking pin' between upper and lower management (Likert, 1961). Surveys of 400 managers found that the number one problem in strategy execution is the failure to effectively manage change or overcome the resistance to change within the organization (Hrebiniak, 2008).

The second view of middle management in strategy implementation is that middle managers hold dual roles of defining and executing strategies (Floyd & Wooldridge 1997, 1994). The second view holds that middle managers provide upper management with unique clarifications of developing issues (Kuyvenhoven & Buss, 2011). The second view grew out of the reemergence of middle management after cutbacks in middle management in the late 1980s and early 1990s did not benefit companies in the manner expected. During this time middle managers were often seen as protectors of personal self-interests and as 'saboteurs' of policy execution (Guth & MacMillan, 1986).

The third view of middle management in strategy implementation is that middle managers are the recipients and implementers of strategy. Middle managers are "change intermediaries" that interpret and make sense of the strategic change, a role that is critical to executing a successful strategy. Misinterpreting the strategy is a key cause of differences between upper management intentions and strategy implementation (Balogun, 2003).

Entrusting Middle Management

Twenty-Five years of management experience reinforces the idea that a combination of the first and second view of middle management continues to be prevalent in the retail sector. Middle management continues to be resistant to change and upper management still sees middle management as saboteurs, trusted to carry out directives, as long as there is no questioning of the strategy.

A recurring theme has emerged from the present research. Change is inevitable and questioning change is forbidden. The idea that upper management never has bad strategies is laughable. Companies continually implement strategies that ultimately fail. New Coke is the first strategy that comes to mind, but a person has to look no further in recent history than the failed pricing strategy at JC Penney, implemented by new CEO Ron Johnson in 2012 (Mourdoukoutas, 2013), to see there is still a need to challenge the process.

Middle managers hold key roles in t strategy implementation, but acting as "yes" men for upper management should not be one of those functions. Company executives have become enamored with business management books of the past with outmoded concepts of suspect origin hidden within the pages. If top executives cannot escape the past, the time has come for middle managers to lead companies into the future.

Beyond experience and education, top executives drive business using simple books with unoriginal concepts, authors motivated by personal financial gain, authors with suspect ethical standards, business theories that have little academic support, lean theories that are proving to raise concerns about profits at the expense of safety, businesses utilizing identical business models while struggling to survive, and acronyms with origins no one can identify. Against the current backdrop, upper level executives have little reason to fear the middle managers that resist the programs from above, as middle managers appear to be the best qualified resources available to guide corporations into the future.

Chapter 1

The Illusionist

The best laid plans don't always get you laid

The truth is irrelevant. Perception is the truth". If The Boss thinks you are doing a good job, you are doing a good job. If The Boss thinks you suck, guess what? You suck, regardless of the truth. Since perception is the truth, why not craft The Boss's perception to The Illusionist's advantage. You have the power to create your own illusion, The Illusion of Competence.

Though there are hard performance truths like sales results, perception dictates The Boss's opinion of performance. Every action The Illusionist takes at work influences The Boss's perception. Unfortunately, The Illusionist cannot predict the perception outcome of every business interaction, but thanks to The Illusion of Competence, The Illusionist can influence perception in a positive manner.

The Illusionist does not pretend not have an ego. The Illusionist expects to be great, expects the team to be great, and expects results to be great. Interestingly, being number one and being great are not the same thing. Being number one runs contrary to The Illusionist's goal of staying under the radar. The Illusionist is okay with being third through fifth, as long as team morale and team results are at record highs.

The Illusionist knows there are exceptions to every rule, and the exception to being number one is when the team is close to number one without trying very hard. The Illusionist will go for the brass ring when it is there for the taking, just as I did while winning a transition lens sales contest at Visionworks, and just as I did when my Eyemart team already had a strong average ticket before dominating that metric for eight straight months between 2015 and 2016.

The Illusionist is a creative thinker that does not except the status quo. The Illusionist knows every process is important, especially if the process has not yet been identified. In order to implement innovative ideas, The Illusionist knows that processes associated with existing programs have to be followed to the letter when The Boss is reviewing these programs, but when The Boss is not looking, The Illusionist does what is needed, within ethical guidelines, to drive success within the business, regardless of corporate sponsorship.

Companies have bad ideas. The Illusionist's job is to create innovative ideas and execute them in conjunction with company programs good or bid. The Theory of Deep Understanding, discussed later, emphatically stresses that The Illusionist is best qualified to identify and implement innovative ideas that lead to successful operations. Top executives' primary responsibility is to focus on the big picture and get the hell out of the way of day-to-day operations, but since that is beyond the scope of executives' ability, The Illusionist manipulates perception in order to allow operational innovations to take hold.

Company executives claim to get feedback from customers to determine what programs to create and follow on the ground floor. The customer knows as much about operations as the company knows about making Grandma's Special Meatloaf. Famous Footwear forced me to abandon two innovative merchandising programs, Checkerboard Merchandising and the Strike Zone Display program, in the name of customer surveys. Famous Footwear has lost tens of thousands of dollars over the last decade due to clearance write offs and handling costs even though the innovative Strike Zone Display program would have resolved the issue in 2001.

The Illusionist cultivates an environment that puts her direct reports first. The Illusionist is a leader that uses a combination of efficiency and compassion to create teams that perform beyond their scope of imagination. The Illusionist believes every team has the potential for greatness, and The Illusionist is the leader to bring greatness to the forefront.

The concept for The Illusion of Competence had been taking shape between 2005 and 2013. The final piece of the puzzle fell into place while taking a self-study course while finishing up my bachelor's degree in the spring of 2013. The assignment was to pick any business subject and spend ten weeks researching the subject and writing a paper on the findings.

The subject matter I chose was based on conflicts I had seen throughout my career between corporate executives, middle managers, and associates. Executives were sending directives to the frontlines, but associates were not embracing the programs. The concept of the paper passed muster with the professor so I commenced to conducting my research.

I was not prepared for the results I found. I had been kicking this concept around for eight years that something was amiss at the top levels of organizations, and this was my first real effort to determine if my suspicions held merit. I started by researching the background of successful business management/leadership books and their authors. I jumped to what I called "acronym" management, and then management concepts like Six Sigma and lean manufacturing. As I investigated each subject, I found flaws in widely accepted business principles that could not and should not be dismissed or ignored. The paper I wrote and its findings make up the preface of The Illusion of Competence, but the paper really just identified inconsistencies. The Illusion of Competence offers solutions.

Setting customer service standards is also an important element of The Illusion of Competence. The customer might not always be right, but her concerns are always genuine. For this reason, decisions are always made from the customer's perspective. If "no" is the normal response, the response needs to be reconsidered. Customers do not care to have policy quoted. They want the leader to find a solution, not a paragraph in the SOP manual.

Chapter 2

The Corporate Embrace

Innovation occurs on the ground floor, not in the penthouse

Your company needs The Illusion of Competence if the executive team or field managers ever uttered the phrases "It's our way or the highway", "It's the price of admission" or "By the book". These phrases have been repeated by executives throughout my 30 year career at companies including Target, Ross Stores, Famous Footwear, Lenscrafters, Visionworks, and Eyemart Express with one constant. The statements were made to employees that did not support corporate programs designed to increase sales and improve operations, but associates continually resisted programs designed to enhance overall performance. Companies see resistant employees as the problem, ignoring, not caring, or ignorant to company program shortcomings.

Corporate executives mistakenly think position and power are equivalent to a corporate policy mandate, but executives actually stifle innovation by requiring subordinates to adhere to company programs without deviation. Employees that deviate from corporate programs do so because they truly believe a better way has been identified, only to be told to toe the company line. The consequence for such attitudes is twofold. Innovations and programs that employees actually value are quashed while unpopular corporate programs are continually pushed to the forefront, negatively impacting employee morale, ensuring the status quo is maintained until the home office says otherwise while forwarding the next unsupported program.

The Illusion of Competence offers the best of both worlds to executives and associates. The Illusion of Competence requires The Illusionist to follow The Boss's top priorities, beat every deadline, return every phone call, and respond to every corporate directive every time, all the time, in order to maintain The Illusion of Competence. At the same time, The Illusionist improves morale, increases productivity, grows sales, and innovates to her heart's content.

The business community tends to think truly new business concepts are few and far between. I chuckle, remembering Charles Holland Duell, the patent office commissioner, who may or may not have stated in 1899 that there was nothing left to invent (Sullivan, 2015). The business community is just as wrong today as Duell was in 1899, but in the age of "corporate knows best", the business community assumption is par for the "my way or the highway" course.

The Illusion of Competence shatters these assumptions. The Illusion of Competence, new and exciting in its own right, was born out of the vagueness of existing theories, but The Illusionist does not stand alone. Micro-Efficiency theory supports The Illusionist by improving efficiency of processes companies did not recognize interfered with more important practices. The Theory of Deep Understanding clarifies why corporate ideas and The Illusionist's ideals do not align, while also explaining why The Illusionist is best qualified to identify, introduce, and execute innovations that move operations forward. Food Poisoning Theory explains the fleeting nature of customer loyalty and provides insight on the approach to customer interactions.

Companies that embrace The Illusion of Competence do not have to expend time and energy dealing with push back from the field. The Illusion of Competence is a bottom line leadership theory. The Illusionist knows that success is not built on today's transaction, but failure and the customer are capable of walking out the door hand-in-hand and never coming back.

The last link in the chain of command is the only link with the knowledge and flexibility to do what is best for the company. The leader closest to the action is the only leader that can accept or reject company programs when corporate is not looking. Every additional link in the chain, from district manager, regional vice president, to the chief operations officer, is required to toe the company line, stifling innovation in the name of being large and in charge. The Theory of Deep Understanding postulates the farther an executive is from ground floor operations, the less the executive understands how to improve operations. Furthermore, the executive will not comprehend The Illusionist's solutions potential to improve operations unless the executive has attained the same level of deep understanding.

Corporate innovation is far from a two-way street. Instead, corporate operational innovation is more of a cul-de-sac, with executives sending ideas down the street, only to see the concepts circle back without support. The Theory of Deep Understanding defines why associates resist corporate programs and why executives should take a closer look at what associates are doing in place of unsupported directives.

Now for the magic of The Illusion of Competence. Corporate and The Boss have every right to hold The Illusionist accountable for failing to foster the Illusion, and corporate gets to set the top five priorities. Mistake on a deposit, failure to send a report, missed deadline, and in fact, any basic operations function is subject to The Illusion of Competence expectations.

Additionally, corporate and The Boss get to dictate key philosophies that drive success. For example, sales goals, production quotas, quality control, average ticket, store presentation, mystery shops, and a multitude of others fall under The Illusion of Competence sphere of influence. The Illusionist's job is to get the job done, and The Boss's is to let them. The Boss gets to hold The Illusionist accountable for not fostering The Illusion of Competence, and The Illusionist gets to foster The Illusion of Competence anyway she sees fit. The Illusion of Competence is truly the win-win leadership theory of the 21st Century.

Chapter 3

The Boss

If you do something wrong for ten years, doing it for ten years does not change the fact that it is wrong

P erception leadership is the most powerful leadership concept in the business world today (I warned you) because it allows The Illusionist's ideas to co-exist with programs businesses spend billions of dollars on annually to implement companywide. Companies believe successful managers must be following company policies and procedures, reducing scrutiny of nonconforming operations. Executives want to credit company programs for successful operations, and The Illusionist cultivates these perceptions.

The Illusion of Competence operates on a basic premise. Humans are not as complicated as they think. In fact, humans are pretty darn predictable, and The Boss is no exception. When The Boss comes for a visit, she expects the division to be clean. The Boss is then going to have four or five priorities that are usually metric or report driven.

The Boss is going to look at her first priority, cleanliness. If The Illusionist's area, division, or store looks and smells clean, The Boss will relax a little bit as she moves on to the next priority. The Boss's next priority is her baby. The Illusionist knows this priority because The Boss speaks to it all the time. If The Boss's baby is safety and she wants to see The Illusionist's safety meeting notes from last month, The Illusionist produces the meeting notes, even if The Boss has not asked to see them for two years. The Boss relaxes a little more as she starts to realize that her priorities are The Illusionist's priorities, but what about the "God" binder that holds all the important reports? The Illusionist pulls out the God binder and every pertinent year to date report is waiting for The Boss to review. Though The Boss has at least two more priorities, she is done looking as she starts reflecting back on days gone by, sharing experiences she feels are relevant to The Illusionist's development. The Illusionist has a name for this phenomenon, "Glory Days", that signifies The Boss and The Illusionist had a good visit.

Conversely, if the division is not clean, The Boss feels disrespected as her senses perk up while moving on to the next priority. What do you mean the safety binder is incomplete, having not been filled out for the last three months? Now, The Boss's tone changes as she reaches for the God Binder without your assistance. Of course, the binder is not complete. You think the God binder is a waste of time because all the reports are easily found on the computer. The Boss's perception of your performance has completely flipped as she starts digging deeper into the inner workings of your operations, bypassing glory days all together. The perception of your incompetence has been set until The Boss visits again six months from now. During this time, the perception will be reinforced by missed deadlines, unreturned phone calls, and missed email responses.

The Illusionist looks at the scenario from a different perspective. The Boss's perception can be shaped with pledge and pine sol providing sensory overload from The Boss's first step into the store, division, or department. The Illusionist puts an extra spit shine on the area of responsibility because The Illusionist knows perception influences The Boss's attitudes and actions. The safety binder is filled out, not because The Illusionist believes words in a binder do anything to improve safety, but because the company holds this belief. The Illusionist keeps the God Binder current, not because The Illusionist believes transferring data from a 21st century computer storage device to a 20th century outmoded storage device makes sense, but because executives do believe it makes sense. The Illusionist does not fight the system. The Illusionist joins the system in the name of promoting The Illusion of Competence.

Covering The Boss's priorities is a key component of The Illusion of Competence, but there are other bases that need to be covered. If The Illusionist is in a satellite location, priorities from the home office are just as important as The Boss's priorities in maintaining The Illusion of Competence. Failure to meet corporate deadlines, return calls, or respond to emails will cause cracks in The Illusion of Competence and draw unwanted negative perceptions. The Illusionist maintains The Illusion of Competence by meeting every deadline, returning every phone call, following up on every email, covering the top five supervisor priorities, and delivering on every promise, in order to execute The Illusionist's own programs without interference. The Illusion of

Competence's goal is to raise performance to such high levels that by the time executives ask The Illusionist how she does it, The Illusionist's beneficial change processes will be hard to deny or resist.

The Illusion of Competence takes emotion out of the program adherence equation. Middle managers waste time and energy resisting programs that are not going to change just because employees do not like the programs. The Illusionist does not concern herself with why a report needs to be in a binder or an email needs a response. Instead, The Illusionist knows that resistance to company programs draws negative attention, contrary to the goals of The Illusion of Competence.

Emotional intelligence is the ability to interpret, understand, and control your emotions, as well as the emotions of others (Psychology Today, 2016). The Illusion of Competence is an "emotional intelligence" based leadership model with a twist. The Illusion of Competence does not try to improve The Illusionist's emotional intelligence. Instead, The Illusion of Competence relies on the predictable nature of other people's emotional intelligence to craft a perception that converges your skills

as a leader with associates below and executives above.

Chapter 4

Execution

You are the "Change"

vector illustration

S ome people might say, "Why not just do a good job while sharing your new ideas and you will not have to worry about creating The Illusion of Competence", but this a misnomer. Corporations invest time and money into their leadership philosophies. A 2012 analysis found American companies invest almost $14 billion annually on leadership development (Hedges, 2014). The implication is companies expect these leadership principles to be implemented and followed, not challenged by lower level managers and associates who question their validity.

Corporations will continue to introduce and promote programs that are not supported on the front lines while maintaining "price of admission" and "my way or the highway" attitudes. Corporate will continue to view The Illusionist as a conduit of policy, not setter of policy. The Illusion of Competence allows The Illusionist to implement her own programs while corporate believes their own inefficient unsupported policies are being implemented and adhered to as planned, while improving morale and earning respect on the frontlines at the same time.

The Illusionist acts as a buffer between the associates below them and the executives above them. The Illusion of Competence lets employees produce at a level beyond their expectations. At the same time, The

Illusion of Competence requires The Illusionist to prioritize directives from direct supervisors, their bosses, and the corporate office, without fail, all the time, every time.

The Illusion of Competence can best be described in the following manner. Take ten stacks of 10 cards and let each stack represent a store, division, or area of responsibility. Number each stack of cards from 1 to 10, with each stack representing The Boss's and corporate's priorities. In seven of the stacks, put the cards in perfect order from 1 to 10. In the three other stacks, mix the cards every which way. Now have someone check the order of all ten stacks and see how closely the person checks the seven perfectly numbered stacks as compared to the mixed up stacks. The more a stack seems in order, the less scrutiny is given to checking the stack. Conversely, the three mixed stacks will be gone through meticulously to get the stacks into the proper order.

The Illusion of Competence's goal is to create a situation where all the cards are in order every time someone of importance is looking at your operations. Just as a person relaxes and checks less closely when all the cards are in order, The Boss will relax if priorities appear to be laid out in order like the stacks of cards. The Illusion of Competence philosophy takes advantage of humans' inability to process every detail and the brain's ability to fill in the blanks to create the warm and fuzzy perception that all is well.

The Illusion of Competence is a philosophy that has been honed over the last 30 years working in middle management with a wide array of retailers. The beauty behind the Illusion of Competence is that, when executed properly, you truly become competent, even as you foster The Illusion. The Illusionist covers every base The Boss requests, without making mistakes, and without needing reminders, lest The illusion of Competence be shattered. The Illusionist does not support every measure put forth by The Boss, but The Illusionist prioritizes every directive, regardless of feelings about the directive. The Boss needs to believe The Illusionist has her back. Once The Illusion of Competence has been established, The Illusionist can institute her own philosophies with minimal interference.

The Boss assesses The Illusionist's performance on bottom line results, attention to detail, timely response, prioritization, and a few "report" driven metrics. In retail, district managers get to their individual stores anywhere from once every two to four months. The district manager will likely spend six hours in the store on any given visit. Since six hours every two to four months is not enough time to accurately assess The Illusionist's performance, district managers rely on reports to assess the health of operations. These reports are your typical financial reports like P&Ls and dashboard reports that track a variety of performance metrics.

The Boss can only have so many priorities on a visit, because the day is only so long. As a result, The Illusionist only needs to cover five bases at the most during a visit. If those bases are covered, The Boss will stop looking, likely well before the fifth priority. If The Boss finds an early priority lacking, she will keep digging. Execute The Illusion and she will stop looking, and perceive The Illusionist is doing a great job.

The Illusion of Competence covers all aspects of management, from operations to employee development. An The Illusion of Competence expectation is that improvements in operations at the micro level allow for more time to coach and develop associate skills. The Illusion of Competence also extends to all leadership interactions, ranging from associates, peers, superiors, and customers. As The Illusion of Competence takes hold in these different capacities, overall performance measurably improves.

While working as a store manager for Famous Footwear, I used to say:

"A store manager needs to be smarter than a shoe box, but you would not believe how often shoe boxes give managers a run for their money".

Employees, whether leaders or associates, do not know how to efficiently do micro functions because they are taken for granted day after day. Employees need to be taught the efficient way to count and manage a till, when and how to use a dolly, and how to efficiently handle cardboard after processing freight. Additionally, subsystems within specific tasks need to be identified and improved. If employees are not taught these functions, not only are the processes done inefficiently, the processes become isolated and subject to The Second Law of Thermodynamics, resulting in extreme inefficiency. But why are learning these processes important? Simple; every advancement in Micro-Efficiency results in more time focusing on customer service and employee development. The Illusionist needs to look at these "taken for granted" processes and determine the most efficient procedures. Identifying and improving micro-processes make employees jobs easier while the additional coaching makes employees better at their jobs. He Illusionist can then implement additional ideas to more receptive ears.

The Illusionist's role in the eyes of top executives is to implement and execute policies and procedures as directed. The Illusionist has this role because top executives do not believe The Illusionist has the skills to do much else. So what is the secret? You have to be The Illusionist because the powers that be think you do not have anything of value to offer to the company. In fact, the company is counting on your lack of skill and originality to help programs filter down to lower level associates. The reason these directives will reach their final destination is because middle managers are not skilled enough to alter the existing programs or develop their own. If not for the divine guidance of corporate gurus, nothing would ever get accomplished. In short, the secret is that executives are counting on your lack of skill to contribute to the company's success.

A popular performance review measurement is called "challenge the process". The idea behind challenging the process is to not accept the status quo as directed by company policy and procedure, but let me be very clear. The company did not spend its share of $12 billion annually on leadership development for middle managers to challenge the process. Middle managers are expected to strictly implement and follow the process. Managers that challenge the process are the same managers that become known as "difficult" or "lacking buy-in", two circumstances that do not bode well for leaders seeking future opportunities within the company.

The Illusion of Competence allows The Illusionist to analyze, improve, or change the process without top executives knowing the process is being challenged. The Illusionist implements innovative ideas side by side with existing programs without looking like part of the problem. In fact, The Illusionist can identify problems and solutions without executives realizing there is a problem. Even if The Illusionist's innovative ideas are not adopted at the corporate level, like innovations created throughout my career, The Illusionist builds a competitive advantage in her sphere of influence by improving morale, efficiency, coaching and development, and customer service.

Chapter 5

The Illusion and subordinates

Associates must be given every opportunity to succeed prior to deciding they have failed

The Illusion of Competence is an excellent change agent leadership two pronged strategy to improve operations. The first strategy is to shape the perception of The Boss and corporate executives. Simultaneously, The Illusion of Competence uses three clearly defined tenets to gain the support of associates within The Illusionist's sphere of influence. Just as The Illusionist can shatter The Illusion of Competence by failing to deliver results, focus on The Boss's priorities, and not respond to corporate directives, associates can shatter The Illusion of Competence when they do not support The Illusionist's change strategy.

The Illusionist raises associate morale by acting as a buffer between corporate and associates, as opposed to acting as an extension of corporate. The Illusionist is not "by the book". Instead, The Illusionist likes to say she has read the book, but is not beholden by the book. Programs that make sense and contribute to success will be followed, but programs that interfere with successful operations and hurt morale will be tabled, only to be dusted off in the name of fostering The Illusion of adherence when The Boss is monitoring operations.

For example, The Illusionist cannot support transferring computer information to paper by hand, whether numerical or informational. For example, companies often have associates transfer sales information to pamphlets, believing writing numbers on paper increases understanding and relevance. The associate doing the writing sees an additional task on top of other tasks of suspect value.

The Illusionist did not say she would not fill out the pamphlets. The Illusionist said she would not support the process. Not only will the pamphlets be filled out in their entirety, altered pen colors will be used from day-to-day to foster The Illusion that the paperwork is filled out on a regular basis.

Associates appreciate The Illusionist's acknowledgement that corporate programs adversely affect ground floor operations. The appreciation increases after The Illusionist introduces programs that make jobs easier for associates. The Illusion of Competence emphasizes efficiency at scales that escape executives and associates, creating increased time for associate development and improved customer service.

Consistent coaching and development contributes to The Illusion of Competence second tenet of making associates better at their jobs. Employees that are better at their jobs provide better customer service and gain a competitive advantage within the company and against outside rivals. The Illusionist introduces structure to processes that corporations take for granted, putting employees in a better position to succeed.

The Illusion of Competence third tenet is to make a personal sacrifice of which associates are aware. Associates feel taken advantage of on a regular basis. A personal sacrifice, combined with making jobs easier and improving operations, provides associates with the feeling The Illusionist genuinely cares about their needs. The Illusionist not only expects loyalty for her efforts, she specifically asks for loyalty in return for cultivating a culture of success.

The Illusionist does not lead by committee. Associate input is appreciated and analyzed for effectiveness, but The Illusion of Competence focuses on improving operations, not empowering associates. The Illusionist has specific strategies to foster positive results, and takes associates along for the ride.

Chapter 6

Micro-Efficiency

If you treat a task like a no-brainer, when finished, the task will look like it was completed by someone with no brains

The Second Law of Thermodynamics simply says that within an isolated system, any ordinary process within the system degenerates to an increased state of disorder (Lucas, 2015). The Illusion of Competence dictates that every process taken for granted on a day-to-day basis, in effect, becomes an isolated system, and as such, is subject to the Second Law of Thermodynamics. Additionally, any task within a process that is not exposed to coaching becomes an isolated system, subject to The Second Law of Thermodynamics. The Second Law of Thermodynamics is the reason associates count coins like they are being dropped into a pachinko machine. The Second Law of Thermodynamics is the reason an employee can't seem to get the right change from the bank. The Second Law of Thermodynamics is the reason a company the size of Eyemart Express does not have the ability to order a dolly to move freight and trash. The Second Law of Thermodynamics is the reason there are always employees that do not know how to ask a customer for a one dollar bill in order to give the customer a five so the employee can save their ones. The

Second Law of Thermodynamics is the reason associates slowly count change back to customers. The Second Law of Thermodynamics is the reason a cashier busts open a roll of dimes, even though there are 35 nickels in the cup next door, leaving the night manager to count 49 extra coins long after the cashier has gone home. Lastly, The Second Law of Thermodynamics explains why virtually all associates know how to vacuum without instruction, because their moms trained associates on vacuuming long before they joined the workforce.

The Second Law of Thermodynamics identifies the problem. Micro-Efficiency is the solution. The Illusionist uses Micro-Efficiency to identify closed systems and subsystems within operations and provides direction that allows these processes to escape The Second Law of Thermodynamics' clutches. My experience with Micro-Efficiency and The Second Law of Thermodynamics is retail industry centric, but micro level inefficiency permeates industries from the manufacturing plant to the office cubicle.

An associate that is never trained on closed system tasks is destined to complete those tasks at the highest level of inefficiency. Additionally, the tasks will continue to languish in a state of wasted time and effort until The Illusionist identifies a structured way to complete the tasks; however, identifying the task does not guarantee optimum efficiency.

Now for the other half of the illusion of Competence. You better have some good ideas and some good coaching techniques, but where do you find good ideas. In order to generate improvements in operations, The Illusion of Competence relies, in part, on Micro-Efficiency. Micro-Efficiency is the process of improving efficiency of mundane tasks associates take for granted. The more efficiently a company completes basic everyday tasks, the more time the company has to focus on customer service and tasks that truly matter. Micro-Efficiency improves efficiency in every aspect of operations.

Cardboard handling is an obvious source of inefficiency I have witnessed throughout my career. A common method is to break the boxes down and lay them down on either a pallet or a flat cart. This method is fine when the mode of transportation is standing still, but as soon as the pallet or flat cart moves, boxes start sliding off, limiting the quantity that can be moved. In "big box" stores, shopping carts are a good method of breaking down and transporting boxes, but the shopping cart is still limited by capacity.

The Illusionist uses the "box in a box" method. In addition to empty boxes, the technique requires just a dolly. Essentially, one big cardboard box is used to hold the other broken down empty cardboard boxes, which are usually folded in half before being placed in the larger box. Once the larger box is full, it can be moved via dolly, or if the quantity being moved is excessive, another empty box can be placed over the top of the first box, creating a new flat surface to start the process all over again. This can best be described as the "box in a box-box on a box" program. This process helps keep the work area clean and allows a large number of empty boxes to be transported without concern of the boxes falling off the flat.

The Illusionist is the key element in this program, recognizing there must be a better way to handle cardboard than leaving the process to associates' designs. The dolly, 55 gallon trashcan, and the box-in-box cardboard method can be combined, allowing a single associate to move large volumes of trash quickly and efficiently. The Illusionist knows that improvements in freight processing and trash handling provide additional time for more meaningful processes like coaching and development.

The Illusionist does not allow dimes in her stores. More specifically, The Illusionist does not get dime rolls from the bank. Do you know what two nickels are? That's right, a dime, but why dimes are inefficient. A roll of dimes has 50 coins, while a roll of nickels has 40 coins. When dimes are eliminated, there are automatically fewer coins to count. Additionally, the lack of dimes means more nickels are used, again ensuring fewer coins to count between shifts.

Eliminating dimes saves a company with ten tills a conservative five minutes per till per week, resulting in 50 minutes a week saved in payroll. Keep in mind that tills are often counted several time a day to accommodate shift changes and opening and closing procedures. If a company had 1000 stores, also with ten tills, the savings are considerably higher. Instead of saving 50 minutes a week in payroll, the company is saving 50,000 minutes, or 833.33 hours. At $12 an hour, your company would save $9996.96 per week and just under $520,000 annually, just by eliminating dimes. Companies like Macy's, Target, and Dillard's have 50 to 100 tills per store, resulting in savings of $2.5 to $5.1 million annually.

I do not contend money saved on payroll by eliminating dimes ends up in company coffers. The real saving is in time that can be directed at more meaningful endeavors like employee development. In fact, Micro-Efficiency's goal is to take the time saved in various closed systems around the company and apply it to employee coaching and development, tasks that are often lacking due to time constraints.

Managers fail because they are inefficient. Workloads are like waves. The Illusionist is efficient at scales that are consistently overlooked in the business world, allowing The Illusionist to ride the wave and stay on top of the workload. In contrast, inefficient managers have the workload crash over the top of them, leaving leaders unable to find the time to focus on priorities, like customer service, that will help the business succeed. The key to The Illusion of Competence in day-to-day retail operations is "efficiency", but not in the traditional sense of the word.

Micro-Efficiency takes on even greater importance in today's business environment. Companies add new programs all the time. The problem is old programs are not fazed out with equal zeal, resulting in increased workloads and decreased time to deal with them. The Illusionist reclaims some of that lost time and redirect it to other areas that need attention.

The Illusionist knows inefficiency steals time from every corner of operations, leaving limited time for employee development, the most important aspect of

The Illusion of Competence. The Illusionist uses Micro-Efficiency to steal time back and redirect it towards associate coaching and development. Micro-Efficiency focuses on everyday tasks, every day, providing a steady stream of cost savings.

Though I worked primarily in retail, time in manufacturing showed the need for Micro-Efficiency can be identified and utilized in operations including manufacturing, logistics, office environment, and retail. The Illusionist knows tasks are completed without thought or training in every operation. Micro-Efficiency tasks are easy to identify because The Boss never identifies them. Any task that is done without identification, training, or thought becomes isolated and subject to The Second Law of Thermodynamics, and benefits from Micro-Efficiency improvement. Instead of ignoring the task, The Illusionist analyzes the task, knowing the function currently resides in a maximum state of inefficiency. The more tasks identified, analyzed, and enhanced, the greater the payroll time savings. Micro-Efficiency is equivalent to compounding daily interest. Micro-Efficiency compounds time savings on a daily basis, providing cost savings that can be redirected to coaching and development.

The Illusionist's job is to identify these tasks, which is relatively easy, and figure out how to improve the processes moving forward. Certain tasks are almost always done without direction or thought of the need for improvement. These actions are not identified as tasks, but are a daily drain on time and money. For example, tills are counted every day, but how many leaders take the time to demonstrate the proper way to count, maintain, and manage a till? Better yet, how many leaders are aware there is a proper way to count, maintain, and manage a till? The answer is abundantly clear every time an associate drops coins into a till like a pachinko machine, day after day.

Counter intuitively, Micro-Efficiency plays a central role in improving associate performance. Leaders often complain of insufficient time to implement and execute corporate directives. The Illusionist uses Micro-Efficiency to improve time management of everyday isolated system and subsystem tasks, freeing The Illusionist to improve other processes and provide real coaching and development to enhance associate performance. The Illusionist finds time hiding in plain sight to not only complete corporate programs, but also develop alternative programs that improve operations and allow associates to exceed company expectations.

The Illusionist takes no processes for granted. The Illusion of Competence mantra is to identify and implement new processes side by side with corporate programs that are deemed good enough by corporate executives. Associates that learn improved processes are, by definition, better at their jobs. I taught multiple employees at multiple companies the best dispense, repair, and adjustment program in the industry, allowing them to raise their customer service level. I created an Excel spreadsheet that identified associate sales strengths and weaknesses, allowing me to specifically coach associates to improve performance. Micro-Efficiency provided the time to create these and many other innovations.

Associates that are not trained on the proper way to take out the trash, break down cardboard, move boxes, process freight, count tills, handle money, use "Ten Key", get change from the bank, use a dolly, or countless other functions, will complete these tasks at the maximum level of inefficiency. The longer the task goes without instruction; the greater inefficiency is ingrained in operations. The Illusionist focuses on these tasks, knowing that doing so pays immediate and future dividends in corporate efficiency and employee development.

Chapter 7

The Theory of Deep Understanding

You know not of what you speak, and speak not of what you know

The Illusionist has a great idea that superiors do not seem to grasp. In fact, The Illusionist has had several great ideas that did not gain traction at the highest levels of the company. There are a number of reasons for this situation to occur, primarily based on The Illusionist's penchant for identifying solutions that run counter to the corporate programs based on the billions spent on leadership development, but there is another reason discovered while finishing my masters' degrees. I call the concept "The Theory of Deep Understanding".

I took a course on innovation at Grand Canyon University in the spring of 2016. One week was spent studying a company called IDEO. IDEO specialized in innovation, mainly through the improvement of existing products. One method used by IDEO was called the "Deep Dive" where a team studied a product, looking to gain in-depth understanding of the product and its use, in order to identify opportunities for improvement based on deep understanding of the product (Morrison, 2010).

That week, a fellow student asked me in a discussion forum how she would know she had reached a state of deep understanding. In order to identify a solution, I had to analyze subjects of which I had a deep understanding. I thought about the question for a day before answering the question.

There are two subjects I can confidently claim fall within the realm of deep understanding. I set the world's record on the arcade game "Asteroids" in the summer of 1981, stretching a game to 55 hours and 3 minutes on a single token. The other subject is racquetball. I have played racquetball for thirty years, winning five New Mexico state titles along the way. When I looked at racquetball and Asteroids, I realized the deep understanding of both subjects had something in common.

I started playing Asteroids about a year and a half before setting the record between July 29th and August 2nd, 1981. I know gamers will immediately go to the defunct Twin Galaxies web site and see that my name is nowhere to be found. Twin Galaxies was not on my radar as a fifteen year old. Instead, the owners of PB Wizard in Scottsdale, AZ, the place where I set the record, contacted

Atari to get the ground rules for the record attempt, which focused on time played as opposed to score. As a consequence, I focused on topping 50 hours on a single quarter. At the back of The Illusion of Competence, you will find my official high score certificate, a newspaper article, and a picture from the Scottsdale Progress of the record attempt. The newspaper article at the time said that I played the game almost subconsciously, leaving me free to eat, drink, and talk to friends, a comment that helped unlock the secret of The Theory of Deep Understanding.

I have had tremendous success playing racquetball, winning five New Mexico state titles and reaching the open division final twice after the age of 40. As a result, players often sought my advice about their games. More than once, players have talked about their thoughts during a shot, to which I would reply that if they were thinking about a shot, they were not playing enough. Reflecting back, I realized that I did not think about my shot when playing racquetball, just as I did not think about Asteroids when playing the game.

With this information, I responded back to the fellow student, "You have achieved deep understanding when you no longer have to think about the subject". Continuing in the discussion group, I expressed frustration that bosses above me did not seem to grasp the significance of ideas I presented to them. The professor responded back that he had similar experiences in academia. The professor went on to say that I should let him know if I cracked the code as peers sometimes just did not get it.

Though the professor was joking, I took his challenge seriously and went to work, cracking the code two days later. I emailed the professor that the reason he was having a hard time getting peers to understand his point of view was that he no longer had to think about the subject, but his peers were still thinking about it, resulting in a disconnect between the two. I call this solution "The Theory of Deep Understanding".

When The Illusionist has a deep understanding of business, The Boss still thinking about the subject will not comprehend the idea, no matter how much The Illusionist tries to get The Boss to understand. The Boss will only understand and except an idea when she too has achieved the same level of deep understanding. The problem is that executives falsely believe they have reached the level of deep understanding, meaning they will never understand the significance of The Illusionist's ideas. Additionally, executives mistakenly associate their success for deep understanding. The Boss is clueless because he stopped trying to reach a level of deep understanding, or worse yet, believes he is already there.

Thanks to experience, education, and insight, I no longer have to think when coming up with business solutions. The answers to problems just kind of hang in space within my mind, coming to the forefront immediately after a problem is presented. Conversely, previous bosses continually failed to understand the significance of my ideas.

When I contacted the CEO of Eyemart Express about my dispensing program, I shot one video and talked about my ideas for two additional videos. I laid out exactly how to get the entire company on the program, including the need to train four or five experts who would then go into the field and teach district and store managers at group meetings how to execute the programs. The store managers would then go back to the stores and train associates while the district managers would have a baseline to judge the implementation and execution of the programs.

The result hanging in front of me to this day is that the first company to successfully implement my dispense, repair, adjustment, and first time progressive wearer program on a company wide scale will have a competitive advantage, allowing the company to advertise and boast about having the best "after the purchase" service in the optical industry. Though I shared this concept with Eyemart and companies I was trying to gain employment from at the time, not a single person I talked to grasped the significance that these after service processes could be standardized to achieve the highest level of service in the optical industry. Eyemart executives did not even ask about the additional videos I envisioned, which covered an additional 75 percent of the program. The Illusionist learns to not get frustrated when ideas and processes are not understood or discouraged outright. The Boss is not the one at fault. The Theory of Deep Understanding dictates that The Boss will not understand until he reaches the same level of understanding.

The Illusionist must introduce innovations side by side with existing programs, because to do otherwise risks exposing the lack of deep understanding at higher levels of the company. The Illusionist's goal is to continue to innovate and reach a level of success that makes her ideas impossible to ignore. Success has a way of getting executives to accept ideas, even when they have not reached the same level of deep understanding.

Executives commonly mistake making money and having an executive title as evidence of their business savvy and knowledge, but these concepts are seriously flawed. Top executives might understand business at macro scales, but true innovation occurs at the front line micro level, an area most top executives never experienced, especially when hired into a new company. The farther an executive is from the nuts and bolts of operations, the less understanding The Boss has of the significance of concepts introduced by subordinates. Even the name "subordinates" has a connotation of keeping lower level employees in their place.

The Theory of Deep Understanding explains why directives from above are viewed as out of touch and why concepts from below are viewed as employees being part of the problem instead of the solution. The farther The Boss is from day-to-day operations, the farther removed The Boss is from The Illusionist's deep understanding.

During three years of Eyemart employment, the area manager above me and the district manager above him offered zero ideas that contributed to advancing my development or that of my associates. Directives were vague at best and confusing at worst. The Ultimate Dispense program was so bad that I was compelled to introduce my own program, even though I knew the program gave my team a competitive advantage over other stores. Keep in mind that I introduced my program the first week on the job. Eyemart was close to its 25 year anniversary when the company rolled out its program, a time gap I find hard to fathom.

Conversely, over the course of three years, I created a sales structure that improved all of my employees' performance. I bought a dolly, a concept foreign to the company at large. I introduced The Illusion of Competence, Micro-Efficiency Theory, Food Poisoning Theory, The Theory of Deep Understanding, as well as The Ultimate Dispense 2.0, the Excel coaching tool and Plus One staffing. These changes improved all facets of operations and allowed my associates to break every relevant sales record set before my arrival. Top executives continually ignored every innovation I shared with them, leaving me to implement the programs on the down low.

Eyemart Express went 25 years and grew to almost 200 stores without seeing the need to supply stores with dollies. As The Illusionist running a store in the smallest building in the company, the need for a dolly was apparent within minutes of leading the store. When I discovered potentially no stores had a dolly, I forwarded two pictures of the dolly in action at my location to the

CEO of the company, thinking that showing the need in a $1.5 million store would make the need obvious in stores that were twice the size and producing twice the sales volume. The email and pictures were ignored by the CEO and executive team, leaving my store as the only store in the company using a dolly to move large case packs of complementary cases to and from the stock room, combine trash and cardboard into large single loads that easily moved from the store to the trash bins, and eliminate the inefficiency and physical strain associated with treating employees like human pack animals. I also expressed the need for quality training on dolly use, knowing the lowly dolly was subject to the Second Law of Thermodynamics and in need of Micro-Efficiency training.

The idea behind a dolly in all stores stemmed from Eyemart's goal to grow to 400 stores over a five year period. I felt the company should make the dolly a standard necessity as part of the new store opening procedure, just like tables, chairs, and computers. Additionally, existing stores would also receive a dolly and required training.

The lowly dolly is one of the hardest workers in an organization. The dolly never calls out sick, never complains, and can lift 600 pounds. And just like other entropy tasks, employees need quality training to experience the full benefits of dolly use. Otherwise, the dolly will be added to the entropy pile. Though there was no denying the need and benefit of supplying dollies for the stores, my email and pictures were ignored by the CEO and other executives, spurring further analysis and contributing to the development of The Theory of Deep Understanding.

In another example, I created an Excel coaching tool at Eyemart Express that added tens of dollars to the store's average ticket and increased commissions for all my associates. The spreadsheet was created from the existing POS system with zero modifications. I simply exported the information to Excel and created a pie chart that measured sales performance more extensively than Eyemart's existing performance tool. The POS system was in existence for years before I was hired, and technically, anyone could have created the tool, but no one in the company came up with the coaching tool after applying The Illusion of Competence principles.

I shared the coaching tool with the CEO, COO, three regional managers, my district manager, and my area manager. Outside of one regional manager that mentioned the coaching tool on a weekly conference call, Eyemart again ignored a tool that made employees better at the store level. My store consistently had one of the highest average tickets in the company, but no executives acknowledged the value of the coaching tool or inquired as to how the store consistently outpaced the corporate average ticket by $40. The inability of top executives at Eyemart Express to recognize or accept the significance of innovative concepts like Ultimate Dispense 2.0, the Excel coaching tool, the benefits of a dolly, combined with a course on innovation at Grand Canyon University, led directly to The Theory of Deep Understanding.

In another eye opening example, I got the sense shortly after starting at Eyemart Express that something was amiss on the doctor side of operations in the store. I had put new programs in place during the first month, but results were not meeting my expectations, based on increases in eye exams coming out of the doctor side not resulting in measurable sales increases. Qualitatively, I knew there was a direct connection between doctor eye exams and retail eyeglass sales, supported by the fact that virtually every eyeglass store has or wants a doctor office next door; however, store sales did not reflect the increase in eye exams.

Quantitatively, a linear regression will support a connection that is qualitatively known to be true. Knowing this, I ran multiple linear regressions in an Excel spreadsheet covering two months of exams and sales information of which I questioned the validity, as well as multiple months prior to when I was hired that did not raise accuracy concerns. Every linear regression I ran on months prior to being hired supported the connection between exams and sales. Conversely, the linear regression ran on the two months I had doubts about showed no connection whatsoever between exams and sales.

Armed with the linear regression results, I shared my findings with my area and district manager in a face-to-face meeting. As I shared the significance of my findings, the boss' eyes glazed over. The two men had no idea what I was talking about as I explained the numbers. As a result, the bosses did not believe my results. A week later, the office manager that supplied the numbers I questioned was arrested for embezzling a rumored $50,000 over the previous three years. The woman had been stealing for three years without concern for being caught. As The Illusionist with a deep understanding of operations, I knew something was wrong less than two months after being hired. My bosses, farther from the flame, did not believe what they could not understand, just as The Theory of Deep Understanding predicts.

The Illusionist that understands The Theory of Deep Understanding does not expend excess time and energy trying to figure out why corporate heads do not understand new and innovative concepts. Instead, The Illusionist builds upon her competitive advantage, setting the goal of doing so well corporate will not be able to ignore the results. The Illusionist has a large toolbox of ideas that cultivates an environment of innovation and success.

The Theory of Deep Understanding is the logical way to explain the disconnection between the frontlines and top executives. The Theory of Deep Understanding dictates that top executives and other superiors will not understand or appreciate The Illusionist's innovative ideas unless they too reach the same level of deep understanding. The Illusion of Competence allows The Illusionist's innovative ideas to exist in the face of corporate rejection and co-exist with out of touch corporate programs. Additionally, executives that embrace The Theory of Deep Understanding will be motivated to expand their own horizons while also paying closer attention to The Illusionist's point of view.

Chapter 8

Food Poisoning Theory

Successful business is built on the customer that comes back tomorrow, not the customer here today

went to Taco Bell 30 years ago. After my meal, I got sick for three days. Needless to say, Taco Bell was eliminated as a food choice for the next three years. Food Poisoning Theory, a key component of The Illusion of Competence, dictates that customers are only as loyal as their last transaction, a circumstance that plays out every day between companies and customers around the world.

Companies throughout the writing of The Illusion of Competence have learned the hard way that programs designed to build loyalty, whether reward based, customer centric, or social consciousness, are only as successful as the last controversy. Target donates millions to local schools annually, but customers could not abandon the company fast enough when 40 million customer credit card accounts were hacked during the holiday season of 2013, contributing to net income falling 46 percent in the fourth quarter of 2013 (Malcolm, 2014).

Whole Foods, a Servant Leadership company, fell on hard times in 2016. Store sales fell due to competition from low price options like Walmart and traditional grocery stores (Oyedele, 2016). Once these retailers started carrying similar merchandise at a lower price, no level of customer servant leadership was able to reverse the trend, resulting in Whole Foods opening Whole Foods 365, designed to attract millennials with high tech and low prices (Fortune, 2016).

Chipotles, a popular servant leadership company, found no loyalty when customers were poisoned at locations around the country. The company held several training sessions and gave away millions in free food, but continued to struggle financially throughout 2016. The efforts were an attempt to reverse a slide in stock value, as well as the perception that Chipotles food handling was unsafe (Kell, 2016).

A basic premise of Servant Leadership is that the Servant Leader puts the needs of others first, without expectation or reciprocation, but this does not hold true. Servant leaders and servant leadership companies expect loyalty from associates and customers for their efforts, but expecting loyalty flies in the face of Food Poisoning Theory. The Illusionist trades personal sacrifice for loyalty, explaining why employees need to be aware of The Illusionist's personal sacrifice.

The Illusion of Competence is not burdened with Servant Leadership assertions. The Illusionist knows the line between the last transaction and the next transaction is not blurred. In fact, the two lines are one and the same, requiring every transaction be viewed as the last transaction.

The customer is not always right, but her concerns are always genuine. The Illusionist knows quoting policy does not build business and is just one of many forms of Food Poisoning. The Illusionist treats every customer interaction based on its own merit, knowing that a solution founded on the customer perspective is a key way to avoid Food Poisoning.

Any and every bad customer experience can lead to Food Poisoning. The Illusionist's primary customer service responsibility is to not give customers Food Poisoning. For example, a customer that comes into the store with an issue can experience Food Poisoning if the solution involves spending more money. The customer might pay the price today to resolve the issue, but the negative experience can lead to Food Poisoning, impacting the customer's decision to return to the store.

The Illusionist operates on a premise called "Plus One", scheduling one more associate than customer needs would dictate. The Illusionist's customer service focus is to avoid situations that can lead to Food Poisoning. The Plus One model improves customer service by avoiding another common cause of Food Poisoning, shorthandedness, while also increasing sales.

Sales are static by nature, meaning associates are only going to individually produce so many transactions per year. In retail, the only real way to consistently increase sales is to increase the number of associates dedicated to sales. The Plus One model consistently provides extra coverage, prevents Food Poisoning, and stimulate year-over-year sales growth.

The Eyemart I took over in 2014 was overwhelmed with customers, with ten to fifteen people regularly waiting for service at any given time. The first strategy to get the store under control and make employees' jobs easier was to reduce the number of customers needing repairs and adjustments to their glasses. The plan was to improve the dispensing process to the point that the customers' need to return to the store for repairs and adjustments abated. I did this by adding a sense of structure to dispensing glasses that had previously been lacking. The dispensing program had only been in place for a month before associates noticed a change in customer traffic patterns.

The dispensing program carried over to repairs and adjustments, with minor modifications. The program allowed employees to complete dispense, repair, and adjustment procedures from a position of confidence, a training method also used in other customer service and selling techniques. Lastly, the program laid out a structured way to teach first time progressive no line bifocal wearers how their glasses worked. The program made employees better at their jobs, made their jobs easier, and helped prevent customers from getting Food Poisoning.

Personal Sacrifice
The only thing I ask is an honest effort

Making a personal sacrifice of which associates are aware is an important change management tool. The Illusionist knows respect is earned, not given. Making a personal sacrifice that benefits associates is a way to build trust when implementing change. A personal sacrifice is of little value if associates are not aware of the significance of the effort. The Illusionist is not shy concerning efforts to benefit associates, knowing that buy-in and morale are key components when building a culture around success.

I worked at three jobs where my personal sacrifice was to forego commissions in favor of quarterly bonuses, but making monetary sacrifices is not a common leadership practice. I was one of only two general managers in my region at Eyemart that consistently avoided commissions, with the fellow manager following my example late in my Eyemart tenure. The Illusion of Competence requires a special type of leader who genuinely cares about associates and customers.

Fortunately, sacrifices do not strictly need to be monetary.

Scheduling is another area where The Illusionist can make a known sacrifice. The Illusionist will close every Friday night or work every Sunday if doing so benefits assistant managers and associates. The Illusionist's goal is to gain buy-in for change while also building goodwill and trust with teammates. As a retail manager, I closed every Friday night over a fifteen year period, knowing fellow managers appreciated being home with family or being out with friends on a Friday night. In return for my sacrifice, I asked for and received an honest effort.

Generally speaking, the same metrics companies use to measure performance can be used to measure honesty of effort. If the team is ranked at the bottom of the district in a key metric, The Illusionist can successfully argue the team is not putting forth an honest effort when coaching to improve performance.

The Written Word

The written word has a negative impact on The Illusionist's team's morale. The scale of the written word is irrelevant. The complement on the bulletin board is just as damaging as the company wide posting on the culture website. Sooner or later (sooner in my experience), an associate will see the complement of another employee and feel slighted, wondering why their own efforts have not been recognized.

The CEO at Eyemart Express used to send private notes to unsuspecting employees, complementing the employees for their hard work and dedication. This was all well and good until the employees started posting the letters on the culture website, leaving other hard working employees to wonder why they were not similarly recognized. The assumed goal was to lift the spirits of said employees, which I am sure it did, but only at the cost of the morale of employees whose names were not attached to the company letterhead.

The Illusionist does not complement or criticize employees in writing if the format is available for human consumption. The written word is subject to interpretation. Associates will infer tone from the written word, regardless of the written word's intent. The Illusionist complements employees in person, face-to-face. The leader that complements employees in an open forum, invariably misses the contributions of additional employees, resulting in a negative impact on morale.

The goal of the written complement is to boost morale by acknowledging a job well done. The problem is that other associates will always feel there are more jobs well done than complements, resulting in hidden animosity and reduced team morale. When an action is just as likely to have opposite of the desired effect, the merits of the program are called into question.

Written directions are also subject to interpretation. The Illusionist conducts a walk through instead of providing written instructions. The Illusionist knows employees can mess up face-to-face instructions, but the walk through is much more effective than written instructions. Write-ups and corrective action fair little better when assessing employee morale.

Write ups and corrective action are terrible motivators that run counter to The Illusionist's goal of not drawing attention to operations. A manager that relies on write ups to get an employee on track, but has no intention of terminating the associate, needs to realize going to the lowest common denominator will make the situation worse, not better. Write ups lower morale, reduce productivity, and destroy trust. The Illusionist only resorts to write ups when the associate's performance is negatively impacting customer service and other employees. The "no write up" policy requires The Illusionist to come up with more creative ways of handling associate performance issues, enhancing leadership skills in the process.

The Illusion of Competence seems similar to Servant Leadership in regards to employee interactions at times, but there are fundamental differences. The Illusionist's loyalty lies with the corporation at the end of the day. Just like customers and Food Poisoning Theory, The Illusionist knows that employees are not obligated to be loyal to superiors just because Servant Leadership puts associate needs ahead of corporate. The Illusionist tolerates associate idiosyncrasies in the name of flying under the radar and increasing morale. The Illusionist builds loyalty through the three tenets of The Illusion of Competence as employees realize The Illusionist puts associates in the best position to experience success. Most importantly, The Illusion of Competence provides corrective action guidelines that do not fly in the face of the theory, unlike Servant Leadership, which struggles to deal with associates that do not respond to Servant Leadership loyalty expectations in its predicted manner.

Chapter 9

A Brief History of The Illusion of Competence

Positive results are no accident

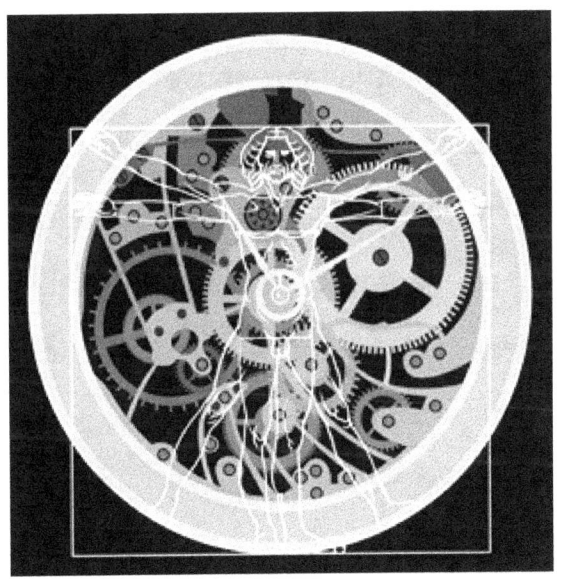

have always been inquisitive as to why things are done the way they are, especially in business. After 25 years in mostly retail management, I started to question the directives of my superiors and the methodologies of my employers. This book is a direct result of this questioning of directives from above.

I started formulating The Illusion of Competence while working as the warehouse supervisor at Target in 1985, though I did not know it at the time. I had many superiors at Target that provided input on warehouse operations, including the warehouse manager, operations manager, merchandise manager and store manager. These managers all had different ideas about how product should flow in and out of the stockroom. I quickly realized that these managers did not respect the complexity of my work. After all, I was just moving boxes around. Initially, my superiors were pulling me in all directions and increasing the difficulty of my job. Eventually, I stopped listening to their directions and started focusing on their end result goals.

I quickly realized that common sense was not all that common, especially at the most elementary levels of productivity. For example, I witnessed the receiving manager at Target pulling pallets of merchandise out to the sales floor with a pallet jack, only to have the pallet tip over and dump merchandise on the floor while turning a corner. I saw this play out routinely from week to week and recognized that there was a logical way to stack products on pallets, but the receiving manager and his employees repeatedly had pallets of merchandise fall apart on the way to the sales floor.

I was promoted to the position of "Hardlines II Area Manager" in 1987. I had extensive autonomy over how to run the seven departments that made up Hardlines II. I learned and developed most of my attitudes toward efficiency during the next three years. I developed a program called "Shortening Your Steps" during this time. The concept was to take a minute while pulling merchandise from the stockroom, analyze where the merchandise was going, and add items to your stocking tub that could be dropped off and stocked while heading to the final destination. The idea seemed simple, but observing employees pushing half full tubs around the store showed that constant analysis of processes was a must in the retail business environment. More importantly, the concept of taking nothing for granted in terms of efficiency analysis took hold during my time at Target, and has been reinforced throughout my career.

Target did not take little things for granted. For example, Target did not keep dimes in its stores during my tenure with the company. I did not understand how much Target saved by eliminating dimes while working for the company, but have since estimated that a company with 1000 stores and 50 tills per store would save conservatively $2.75 million annually in payroll. The savings proportionally go up or down based on the total number of stores and tills on hand. The payroll savings are why The Illusionist eliminates dimes, regardless of the scale of operations.

In another example, Target taught all sales floor employees "ten-key" and the proper till counting method. These two training lessons were designed to improve cashiering efficiency. Interestingly, Target focused on efficiency at smaller scales at the expense of large scale efficiency. Target executives did not respect freight processing, seeing it as necessary to the end goal of reaching the consumer. The Illusion of Competence origins can be traced back to the days of Target not respecting the freight handling process.

Target stores used to get large shipments of pool-side tri-fold loungers. The loungers came in a case pack of six loungers, each individually enclosed in a plastic bag. In order to display the lounger, I would take each lounger out of the box, remove the plastic cover, and put the lounger back in the case, which was used to display the loungers in bulk on the sales floor. Since Target stores received hundreds of cases of loungers every spring, days were spent getting the loungers ready for the sales floor.

One day, I decided there had to be a better way. I stood over a case pack of loungers and started analyzing the process. I soon tried a trick of leaving the loungers in the case and tearing away the plastic covers in quick succession, similar in fashion to a magician quickly pulling a tablecloth out from under a table setting. The plastic pulled off the loungers with ease while still in the case pack. The tablecloth technique left the loungers in the case pack and reduced processing time by 80 percent.

Just for fun, I had an associate process the loungers the old way for about three hours one day before showing him the tablecloth trick. The employee's genuine displeasure at being allowed to be inefficient for hours gave me an indication of the power of efficiency. Reflecting back, Micro-Efficiency was invented the day I discovered the tablecloth trick in the late 80s.

A new store manager took over the location where I worked shortly before I left Target. This new manager ran the store "by the book". I soon discovered the book must have been written for the rest of us because he did things however he wanted while holding everyone else accountable when it came to policy and procedure. I became frustrated as I lost my independence as a manager while the store manager enjoyed his own autonomy. In large part, I left Target in 1989 for this reason, not realizing that the same hypocrisy existed throughout the business world, including my new job at Lionel Playworld.

Lionel Playworld was a "Toys R Us" clone associated with the Lionel toy train family. I was hired as the merchandise manager, but was pointed toward operations after training. As the operations manager, I was in charge of front end register and the cash office, as well as back end receiving and warehouse operations. I could not learn front or back end operations at Target unless I was put in charge of one of those areas so the Lionel Playworld experience paid immediate dividends in terms of my development.

One experience stands out at Lionel Playworld. When I first started, the existing operations manager was a young lady. The store had an audit shortly after I started. The operations manager was in a state of panic on audit day, convinced the auditor did not like her. The first thing the auditor checked was the safe count, which came up five dollars short. The lesson learned was that missing the first question on an audit pretty much guarantees the audit will go poorly. The operations manager blamed the auditor for having a personal agenda, never taking accountability for the bad safe count. Though unknown at the time, the consequences of not executing The Illusion of Competence were on full display that day.

Lionel Playworld announced that our store was closing in the fall of 1991, but I had already secured a new position as an assistant manager at Ross Stores. I spent the first year at Ross as the Merchandise Manager, but switched to operations manager after transferring to a store in Albuquerque, NM. The time at Ross was pretty nondescript as I continued to refine efficiency and administration skills.

The primary lesson learned at Ross was the importance of figuring out my boss' weaknesses and excelling at them. Bosses have been bad at paperwork throughout my career, and Jay, the store manager at Ross, was no exception. The store manager asked me specifically to cover administrative paperwork when I took over as operations manager. The paperwork consisted mainly of cash office tracking and employee file maintenance. A major goal of The Illusion of Competence is to make the boss' job as easy as possible, and understanding the importance of paperwork execution is a key component in putting bosses at ease.

I left Ross Stores in 1995 after not getting the store manager position when the store manager was fired. I spent a short time at MacFrugals and only two weeks as a manager in training at Big 5. Two weeks would seem like too short a time to make an impact at a company, but that assumption would be wrong.

Big 5 was opening two stores in Albuquerque and I was helping with the conversion of one store from a golf shop to a Big 5. Early on, the management team of three managers was designating stockrooms for merchandise. One stockroom held exercise equipment like rowers, weight benches, and the like. Merchandise poured into the stockroom, but quickly choked off to the point where merchandise was stacking up in the hall outside the room.

The store leaders were trying to figure out what to do with the excess merchandise, but I had identified a common mistake from my days as the Target warehouse supervisor. The managers were trying to get merchandise to fit shelving instead of adjusting shelving to fit merchandise.

I came in early the next morning and went to work, taking virtually everything out of the stockroom so I could reorganize the shelving. The shelving units were four foot long by two foot deep set back-to-back in three aisles with a wide array of shelf settings. I started pulling shelves out and creating uniform shelf heights on each aisle, essentially turning the back-to-back units into double sided single units with pass throughs that allowed items to slide from the front of one shelf to the back of the other unit, creating room for bulk items.

I heard through the grapevine the assistant manager was not happy I had emptied the stockroom, but not for long. Properly setting the shelves not only made room for all product left in the hallway, room was left over for considerably more merchandise. The assistant manager went out of his way to apologize, ironically, for what he had said to other employees about me tearing apart the work done the prior day. In a recurring theme, management had underestimated and been outsmarted by a lowly box.

I had interviewed with another company two months before being hired by Big 5. Shube's Manufacturing was looking for a shipping manager to manage 56 employees and eight supervisors, a responsibility level I could not resist. Shube's was run by Scientologists who have their own theories on business leadership.

Most of Shube's Scientology practices did not influence my own theory, but one scientology concept did resonate with me. According to Scientology, a person who's graph is pointing up (don't ask) should be left alone to continue being successful. If a leader had a great performance week, she was beyond reproach. In fact, a person criticizing a leader having a successful run was viewed as a bigger problem than the person being criticized. Though not officially a part of The Illusion of competence, executives could learn at least one thing from scientologists.

The biggest innovation accomplished at Shube's was the reorganization of the shipping division. Shube's had three primary customers including Avon, QVC, and the Home Shopping Network. Shube's shipping room was organized with work stations for these prime customers, but there was no rhyme or reason to their setup. I interceded and positioned the work stations based on volume, with Avon, our largest customer, closest to the shipping doors. I thought my setup was obvious, but I had learned through the years that nothing was as obvious as it seemed. The Theory of Deep Understanding helps explain this phenomenon.

The Shube's plant was struggling when I came on board and continued to do so until I was laid off about two years later. After spending a few months unemployed, I landed the job at Famous Footwear that first planted the seeds of writing The Illusion of Competence.

I started as an assistant manager for Famous Footwear in 1998, and was promoted to store manager six months later. Working at Famous Footwear for seven years was invaluable, not because the company was so good, but because Famous was so inept at virtually every turn and every process. I had never seen a company that was so inept at displaying its own merchandise as Famous Footwear in my thirty years in business. As a result, I invented my own merchandising process called checkerboard merchandising that helped differentiate brands within categories and allowed customers to more easily shop for shoes.

I combined checkerboard merchandising with another concept I invented called strike zone displays. Strike zone was the placement of display shoes at heights between the customers' chest and knees, like the strike zone in baseball. The program ran counter to the Famous policy moving shoe displays and boxes down to the bottom shelves as the shoes sold down, becoming what Famous called short lots.

Famous Footwear treated short lots like red headed step children, shunning them to the bottom shelf or back clearance aisles. I had a different philosophy. Short lots were shoes that were selling, but no longer available for restock. For that reason, I used to keep short lots front and center on the top shelf of display units, the theory being that short lots were popular shoes in search of the right foot size. Make the short lot easier to find and the right size foot would find the shoes. Put a short lot display shoe on a bottom shelf and you had decided you no longer wanted to sell that shoe, creating a monster that Famous struggles to control to this day.

I implemented checkerboard merchandizing and strike zone programs for the first time after being transferred to Sedona to act as a co-manager at a high volume outlet store. Through no fault of the fellow and existing co-manager, the store was in the typical Famous Footwear state of disarray with poor merchandising processes in place; however, I had to take the fellow co-manager's concerns under consideration before implementing major changes. I failed to find a subtle way to convince the co-manager I had a better way, so instead, I implemented checkerboard merchandising and the strike zone display program on the co-manager's day off. The goal was to convert as much of the store as possible before the co-manager came back the next day, and be prepared to explain the benefits.

The co-manager came in the next day and was thrilled with the changes. I found dozens of short lots store employees did not even know were in the store. The look was cleaner, more organized, and easier to shop. The store change was successful because the results were clearly better that the previous procedures. The Illusion of Competence allows The Illusionist to implement effective programs without drawing attention when programs fly in the face of corporate procedures. Executives expect middle managers to follow corporate procedures procedures, not create their own. The time in Sedona was the first real implementation of The Illusion of Competence, though nameless at the time. Soon thereafter, I was cleaning up stores in Arizona, New Mexico, and Colorado.

My district manager recruited me to help clean up a couple stores in the Denver area shortly after I transferred to Sedona. I was part of a team of four store managers assigned to the cleanup task, along with a district manager from Denver offering guidance. A problem quickly emerged when the district manager was too busy to be involved in the cleanup, resulting in a lack of team leadership. In consequence, the team was spinning its wheels while trying to clean up the Castle Rock outlet store, one of the higher volume stores at Famous Footwear.

The team had no leadership, no strategy, and I had no power to change the situation, but I did anyways. I had a strategy and a plan. I implemented a strategy to maximize space and create additional space based on Target's structured merchandising philosophy. The store was overstocked, but my strategy created usable space and greatly improved the store appearance. By the end of the five days, the team effort was described as a success.

I went back to the district manager and told him of the challenges I faced. When two more stores around Denver needed attention, I told the district manager I was happy to help, but based on the challenges I previously faced and the end result, I should be put in charge of the team to avoid similar future challenges. The district manager agreed and turned me loose to, in the district manager's words, "do what I do".

Famous Footwear transferred me to the Albuquerque west side store six months after I moved to Sedona. Multiple managers had failed at the Albuquerque location during the store's first three years. I had mentioned my willingness to move back to Albuquerque while rooming with a store manager from the Albuquerque district while cleaning up a store in Colorado Springs, CO. Three weeks later, I was packed up and on the road to Albuquerque, wondering if I should have been careful for what I wished.

The Albuquerque Famous Footwear was in total disarray, with an average of 80 stolen pairs of shoes a month, including a pair stolen by the previous store manager just weeks after he joined the company. The crew at the Albuquerque store consisted of a 21 year old assistant manager and an eighteen year old part time employee. There were other employees working the store at the time, but the working relationship and friendship built with the assistant manager and part time associate continues to this day.

Though nameless in 1999, The Illusion of Competence and Micro-Efficiency immediately went into full effect. Efficiency wise, the first things I did was introduce the assistant manager and associate to the power of the dolly. The dolly is the hardest worker in the store. It never complains, never calls out, and can lift 600 pounds. The problem is that, unless properly trained, the dolly will be left in the backroom while human pack animals do the heavy lifting.

The Albuquerque Famous Footwear needed to be reflowed as part of the normal seasonal business cycle, allowing me to implement checkerboard merchandising and the strike zone display program. The first day, I watched the assistant manager and associate move shoes by hand, allowing me to demonstrate the value of a dolly and Micro-Efficiency.

The associate immediately took to the dolly, enjoying the increased efficiency and strain reduction from not carrying around shoe boxes all day. The associate told me that previously, shoes were moved by hand during store moves, taking weeks to complete; however, there were still hidden complexities the associate had to learn about using a dolly.

One day, the associate was bragging about how efficient he was moving shoes with the dolly. I told the associate he was doing okay, but had room for improvement. Not understanding, the associate asked how he could improve the process. The associate would grab a load of twelve shoes on the dolly and move the shoes to their new location. The associate would then come back and grab another load and repeat the process. I showed the associate that, with a little planning, he could load a stack of shoes, take them to their new location, load a new stack of shoes at that spot, and move them to their required location, limiting the number of steps taken with no shoes loaded on the dolly. The trick essentially increased productivity by 100 percent, leaving the associate shaking his head and laughing at how easily I demonstrated a more efficient method.

Famous Footwear has a highly inefficient freight program because the company does not want employees to work on freight while the store is open. Though the company goal is to focus on customer service, the repeated handling of shoes prior to reaching their final destination actually distracts from consistently providing quality customer service, especially at a company as payroll conscious as Famous Footwear.

Back in the late 90s, freight boxes were staged on a main drive aisle and processed to their final spot on the sales floor inefficiently by hand or efficiently via the dolly. Now, shoes are removed from their cases in the back room, organized on large metal carts, and then wheeled to the floor where they are processed by hand before or after operating hours.

Just as Famous Footwear forced me to abandon checkerboard merchandising and strike zone display shoes, ivory tower freight processing directives hurt employees at the lowest levels. The only viable solution for a store manager at Famous Footwear to overcome executive lack of understanding is The Illusion of Competence and Micro-Efficiency.

The assistant manager was a tougher sale. Initially, the assistant manager saw me as just another flunky in a parade of flunkies, incapable of teaching him anything he did not already know based on his three years of Famous experience. The assistant manager's attitude changed after seeing sales increases and stolen shoe reductions associated with the changes I implemented.

I came up with several innovative solutions to reduce stolens. The first solution dealt with the assistant manager's attitude toward people he profiled as potential shoplifters. The west side Famous Footwear was in a mall with prevalent gang activity. The assistant manager would greet homies at the door and then look obviously at their feet. The assistant manager and I actually argued in the back room on my third day after I told him that disrespecting gang bangers was a self-fulfilling prophecy that encouraged thefts. The assistant manager said he heard what I was saying, but could not see changing his method. I waved my hand at the 80 plus empty stolen boxes on the receiving room shelving and emphatically stated, "It's not working".

Potential shoplifters would come in the store and associates would play a cat-and-mouse game of "Are you watching me" and "I am not watching you". Popular shoes were common targets for shoplifters, meaning the likely location and destination of the shoplifters could be narrowed down with little effort. Instead of playing security guard on patrol, I stationed associates by the popular shoes before potential shoplifters entered the store. The theory was that this is our store. We do not have to explain what we are doing in our store. We just happen to be doing it next to the shoes thieves want to steal.

The Albuquerque Famous Footwear had 60 feet of floor to ceiling glass across the front entrance, meaning that shoplifters could see the previous "task" focused employees working hard to earn a paycheck. Shoplifters that looked in my Famous Footwear saw four employees inviting them in from various points around the store. The Illusion of Competence and Micro-Efficiency allowed employees to focus on customer service during peak times, forcing shoplifters to reconsider before coming into the store.

The second inventory at the Albuquerque Famous came in at a .57 percent, well below the previous 1.01 percent. I immediately knew the new results were too good, setting a corporate expectation that would be difficult to match. I purposely left a 1.38 percent inventory certificate that earned a previous manager a bonus on my office wall as a reminder when half a percent became the new standard in future years. Like I said, humans are predictable animals.

The effectiveness of the programs I enacted at Famous Footwear were reflected in sales results. The store, hemorrhaging losses when I took over, had the highest sales increase to plan for the district in 2002, 2003, and 2004. Prior to transferring to another struggling Famous Footwear on January 1, 2005, my new district manager asked what I hoped to accomplish at my new location. I told the district manager my expectation was to continue my streak of top sales increases at the new store, validating the processes I had put in place in Albuquerque. The Santa Fe store was twice the size of the Albuquerque store, had broken the previous two managers' spirits, and suffered from poor inventories and sales during its three years of existence, providing a serious challenge to the processes I planned to implement.

Micro-Efficiency was the key to success at the Santa Fe Famous Footwear. Improving processes people take for granted created time needed to provide real coaching and development, not just lip service in the name of corporate policy. Improvements in freight processing, dolly utilization, and administrative functions provided time to focus on customer service and loss prevention. I led the Santa Fe store for nine months before moving on to Lenscrafters in September, 2005. During this time, the Santa Fe store had its best inventory ever and had a strangle hold on the top increase to plan in the district year to date, satisfying my stated goal and validating my methodology.

The Famous Footwear in Albuquerque had a Lenscrafters across the hall. I would be working my ass off daily, only to look across the hall to see four Lenscrafters employees sitting around watching me work. At the time, I made a mental note that given the chance, that was the job I wanted. The new Albuquerque Famous Footwear store manager, my future wife, Lisa, told me Lenscrafters was recruiting her for its Santa Fe store. Lisa could not drive to Santa Fe due to family constraints, but I was already making the drive to Santa Fe, so I applied. I then passed one of the hardest employment tests I had ever faced, a four hour affair that ranked leadership abilities, and was quickly hired after the interview process and drug test. To this day, Lisa says I stole her job.

I was hired as the Santa Fe Lenscrafters general manager with no optical experience. Lenscrafters' executives acknowledged that the Santa Fe location was one of the most challenging stores to run in the company due to a shallow talent pool in Santa Fe and the surrounding area. To enhance the challenge, the Santa Fe store doctor quit after six months and was not replaced during the remainder of my three plus years at Lenscrafters. Finding success in an industry dependent upon doctor prescriptions without a doctor on staff was a challenge worthy of the Illusion of Competence.

There were similarities in the operational philosophies between Famous Footwear and Lenscrafters. Famous Footwear and Lenscrafters appeared to be reading from the same playbook. The more interesting fact was that the programs in place at the store level concerning customer service and the measuring of performance at both companies were seriously flawed in the sense that employees did not like the programs at either company. The striking similarities between the two company's programs, combined with the lack of buy-in from lower level associates at both companies, increased my curiosity about how the store level programs came into being in the first place.

I started developing the most comprehensive dispense, adjustment, and repair programs in the optical industry within months of taking over the Santa Fe Lenscrafters, motivated by limitations of following guidance of my lead optician, who relished and abused his position as the most knowledgeable optician in the store. The lead optician had academic credentials as an optician and 15 years of experience at Lenscrafters. The lead optician used his knowledge power to dictate the actions of other store associates, myself included. I quickly learned the lead optician was a hypocrite, parading around the mistakes of others like a sign carrying cartoon character, while hiding his own errors from unknowing eyes. My program initially was developed for customer eyeglass adjustments, as I tired of relying on the lead optician's biased instructions, but the program expanded over the next ten years to include eyeglass dispensing, repairs, and instructions for first time progressive wearers.

I left Lenscrafters in 2009, starting my college career shortly thereafter. A funny thing happened after I started online classes at Kaplan University. I not only enjoyed college, I excelled in my studies and earned my associates degree in 2011. I kicked around at a couple odd jobs with Wells Fargo and National Vision during this time.

I got my next real job with Eyemasters (now Visionworks) in 2011. I quickly realized that the same issues I ran into at Famous Footwear and Lenscrafters were present at Visionworks. The company had customer service and sales models, but they were not well received by the associates on the front lines. Once more, the company's reaction was to tell associates and store management, "It's our way or the highway". Visionworks' executives saw the associates as the problem, not the sales programs. The main purpose of these programs was to improve sales and employee commissions. Common sense told me "If programs improved sales performance and increased commissions, why wouldn't employees embrace them"? The answer was painfully obvious. Employees did not buy into these programs because the programs did not work, and no amount of threats from a corporate ivory tower was going to change that fact. By coincidence, the programs at Visionworks appeared to be cut from the same mold as Famous Footwear and Lenscrafters.

Culture and The Illusion of Competence are closely related. The first tangible change I made at Visionworks was to create a "Wall of Fame" in the breakroom. The lab manager, asked why I made a wall of fame when the store had never achieved anything of merit during his 20 years at the store. I assured the lab manager that things were going to change.

There was one interesting fact about the lab manager. The district manager told me when I was hired that the lab manager was a problem and asked how I would deal with him. I made it a habit of making my own assessments, so I had no preconceived notions before working with the lab manager. A year after I took over, the previous store manager visited the store. The manager asked me sarcastically how it was going with that guy in the lab. I told him the lab manager would through a wall for me. The former manager's facial expression was priceless.

I just saw the lab manager outside a bank the other day talking to the security guard who I also know. I overheard the lab manager tell the guard that I had just earned two masters' degrees and was the best boss he ever had, high praise for someone I led for one and a half of his 25 year Visionworks career. That is the power of The Illusion of Competence.

The Illusion of Competence was in full effect at Visionworks. Sales at my store were up six percent at the end of 2011, covering the first priority of The Illusion to get positive sales results. In optics, retail associates and lab associates seem to always be at odds. I managed the store from the lab perspective, knowing that the key to on time delivery resided in the lab, not the retail floor. Siding with the lab effectively ended the conflict between the two departments and secured the lab manager's buy-in to future changes.

The Illusion of Competence has three tenets that allow The Illusionist to successfully lead her associates. Make your employees jobs easier, make your employees better at their jobs, and make a personal sacrifice of which your employees are aware. To that end, I introduced my dispense, repair, and adjustment program, which both made jobs easier and made employees better at what they do. I also vowed to never personally sell glasses. Though Visionworks general managers did not earn commission, every pair sold by managers denied employees a commission opportunity.

Micro-Efficiency was also introduced. When I showed the lab manager multiple tricks concerning cardboard processing, he was amazed. I integrated the dolly, trashcan, and cardboard in such a way that trash and cardboard removal processes were streamlined. I greatly improved freight processing by limiting the number of times frames were handled between the case pack and the display cases, doing most of the work myself so my associates could focus on sales. I improved cash handling, setting expectations on till makeup and getting change from the bank. And as I had always done, dime rolls were officially banished from the store.

Superiors and the corporate office were also important elements in The Illusion of Competence success at Visionworks. Every directive from corporate or the boss was delivered on time without error, but also without regard to whether the directives were embraced at the store level. Leaders waste time and energy questioning directives from above, only to raise concerns about company loyalty. On the other hand, meeting every deadline, filing every report, and completing every document allows corporate and The Boss to relax, knowing the store is running as expected.

In the meantime, employees could focus on what they did best, building relationships and improving sales techniques with real time coaching. Since I did not sell glasses, I paid attention to employee sales practices and identified lost opportunities "in the moment" when employees could see that a different approach could have garnered better results.

I ran the Visionworks store for the next 18 months. During that time, the store had the highest increase to plan for the entire company in August, 2011, just three months after I took over operations. The store also tied for highest increase to plan in the district with a six percent increase in 2011. For added measure, the store won a transitions lens selling contest in the spring of 2012, securing a catered lunch for the store. The Wall of

Fame was so covered with accolades by the end of my Visionworks tenure that I had to remove old awards to make room for new awards, including corporate sales acknowledgements and numerous customer cards and letters thanking employees for stellar customer service.

Visionworks executives that visited the store looked specifically at the SERVE customer service model and the documentation used to track the program. As a 21st century leader, I had a problem with my associates hand writing sales numbers in a pamphlet to track progress from week to week when the same information was found in Visionworks' computer operating system. The beauty of The Illusion is that my lack of support for the SERVE program was irrelevant. Visionworks wanted employees to fill out pamphlets with employee sales tracking information, and that is what Visionworks got.

The district manager commented that he appreciated that I held my employees accountable for filling out the tracking pamphlets, and he could tell that the pamphlets were legit because the employees used different pen colors from day to day. I chuckled to myself, knowing that I had instructed employees to use different pens to add legitimacy to documents the team filled out just before important visits. You have to work harder than that to catch The Illusionist.

Employees would put on a "dog and pony" show for executives when they visited the store. The SERVE program was executed from start to finish, satisfying executives' stated desire for conformity from store to store. Employees would then switch to a more natural mode of customer interaction when executives were not in the store.

I left Visionworks in November, 2012, becoming a store manager for Zale's Corporation. I enacted the same concepts at Zale's that were effective in earlier positions. I focused on coaching associates on the methods Zale's used to sell diamonds, helping employees hone their selling skills.

Finding success at Zale's was difficult as my store was a failing Zale's subsidiary known as Gordon's, but there were a couple bright spots. In five months, I developed two employees that consistently ranked in the top five in sales to goal against 70 other associates in the district. The district manager had encouraged me to terminate one of the employees when he hired me, and to this day, acknowledges that I saw something in her that he had missed.

The district manager made me aware in the fall of 2013 that the store lease would expire in the spring of 2014. I left Zale's in October, 2013, not wanting to become a lame duck. I started my masters' programs in November of 2013 and was hired by Eyemart Express in March, 2014

I took over an Eyemart Express store that was out of control, not with employees, but with customers. I went to two interviews at the store prior to being hired, and both times, the store was packed with customers (20 customers waiting for service). After going in to sign paperwork on a third trip to the store, I went to my wife waiting in the car and said, "I don't think I know what I am getting into". Though daunting, I had already formulated a plan prior to officially getting hired.

Against that backdrop of store craziness, I promptly announced when introduced to employees that I was not there to sell glasses, never mind that I earned the exact same commission as the employees. I told employees that I would focus on common functions like dispensing, repairing, and adjusting glasses while employees focused on sales. Employees knew I was literally taking money out of my pocket while lining their pockets with more money, fulfilling the third tenet of The Illusion of Competence to make a personal sacrifice of which your employees are aware.

The first tenet of The Illusion is to make employees better at their jobs. I accomplished this by introducing my dispense, repair, and adjustment program and coaching employees to sell better products. The second tenet of The Illusion is to make employees' jobs easier, accomplished by introducing Micro-Efficiency, though two years away from its official title.

Eyemart had 170 stores when I was hired. I quickly discovered the store did not have a dolly, and there was no way to order a dolly. My store was the smallest stores in the company square footage wise, and it took me a day to know a dolly was a necessity for receiving and stocking case packs of courtesy cases and removing trash and cardboard. I was dumbfounded at the thought that a company 25 years into its existence had not found the need for a dolly. The Micro-Efficiency wheels started churning at the company's scale of accepted inefficiency. I bought a dolly with petty cash within two weeks of being hired, and though I shared the need with top executives, my store continued as the only store with a dolly until my last day of employment.

I did earn a profit sharing bonus, which I felt would be bigger if I got employees in the right frame of mind. Toward the end of my time at Eyemart, the company created a measuring tool that ranked all employees in the district based on various sales metrics. Not surprisingly, general and continually ranked at the top of the list, allowing me to highlight my monetary sacrifice as I set employee expectations. I reiterated to associates that I was the only manager in the region that did not pick their pockets. In return, I expected the employees to have my back and execute sales in the manner that I coached.

The Illusion of Competence allows The Illusionist to implement innovative programs without drawing attention to the methodology before their success can be established. One big innovation I came up with at Eyemart was an Excel coaching tool designed to identify selling strengths and weaknesses. I credited the tool with boosting the store's average ticket consistently $40 above company and district average. I created the tool based on information available in the company's POS system for the previous seven years.

The second innovation was Micro-Efficiency, which included dime elimination, buying a dolly and training on its use, till and cash handling management, and streamlining freight processing. Additionally, Micro-Efficiency dictated every task be reviewed as a potential isolated system or subsystem that could become subject to the Second Law of Thermodynamics.

I created an environment where associates could focus on improving sales processes and commissions. I did repairs, adjustments, and dispenses while associates processed sales. This approach was key to changing the perception the store was always overwhelmed and out of control, a common cause of Food Poisoning.

The third innovation was introduction of the most comprehensive dispense, repair, and adjustment program in the industry. I am not a certified optician, but the assistant manager and one of my other associates were both certified opticians. I also had an employee with five years of Eyemart Express optician experience. I quickly established I was the most knowledgeable optician in the store, especially when interpreting data and troubleshooting glasses. Knowledge power was an important element when seeking buy-in for new programs.

Results speak louder than words. The accomplishments of my Eyemart team bordered on ridicules. In two and a half years, the store had its best day ever twice. The store set records for best week ever twice in February, 2016 during the industry's peak season. The store then had another best week ever in July, 2016 during the second busiest season. The store had its best month ever in February, 2016. The store then had its best month ever again in March, 2016. The store had its best quarter ever in the first quarter, 2016. When I took the store over in March, 2014, sales were already down five percent year to date. The store finished 2014 up 11 percent and had its best year ever. In 2016, the store again had its best year ever with only one holdover associate from my hire date.

The Illusion of Competence was in full effect during this time. I had completed my two masters' degrees in July, 2016. I started writing The Illusion of Competence in November, 2015 and was using Eyemart as a testing ground. Micro- Efficiency was six months from trademark protection in August, 2016, having been named one night in November, 2015 while trying to understand why I repeatedly saw extreme examples of inefficiency at scales that escaped other leaders. I made a connection between Micro-Efficiency and the Second Law of Thermodynamics at that time. I had developed and named Food Poisoning Theory during 2015 and 2016. I had also developed The

Theory of Deep Understanding in the spring, 2016, based on an "Innovation" course at Grand Canyon University. The only thing left to do was to share the most innovative business theory in the history of middle management with you.

Conclusion

So there you have it, the culmination of a journey that started over 30 years ago, without realization I was a journey until 2005. Initially, I just wanted to understand why programs that were rejected at the lowest levels of employment at my old companies were the same programs that were being rejected at my new companies. By the time I saw the same situation at three straight companies, the thought changed from "Something is wrong" to "There has to be a better way".

Don't get me wrong. I spent years challenging the system, pointing out bad ideas as I saw them and finding a better way while doing my own thing, only to be seen as part of the problem in the end. Based on that experience, the new way had to be intertwined with the existing way, at least until the new way had been clearly established as the better way.

By this time, writing a leadership book was a thought, not a real necessity, but that was about to change. The paper I wrote just before getting my bachelor's degree researching various leadership theories exposed numerous shortcomings in many of the prominent leadership theories of the day. Now, I had to write a book, and I had to advance my education in order to add value to my assertions.

To say I am not a fan of Ken Blanchard, The One Minute Manager, Situational Leadership, or Servant Leadership is an understatement. I was in my second conversation with an admissions councilor at Grand Canyon University before discovering Blanchard's name was literally on the side of the GCU Ken Blanchard School of Business. Though it initially gave me pause, I decided tackling my masters' degrees in an environment outside my comfort and philosophical zone would be just the challenge to spur further development of The Illusion of Competence. Attending GCU allowed me to read three Blanchard books and take courses on situational and servant leadership. The insight gained was useful in my personal growth while also acting as a motivator for The Illusion of Competence.

When I started writing The Illusion, there was really only one concept, The Illusion of Competence, a way to manipulate The Boss while doing things the way The Illusionist wants. Micro-Efficiency was purely an observation that employees completed unassigned tasks in the most inefficient possible manner. I had focused on improving these tasks, but I needed more than a statement that I had seen certain tasks consistently done inefficiently throughout my career. I needed a reason.

One night in November, 2015, I was analyzing inefficiency on small scales when I realized the Second Law of Thermodynamics stated isolated systems descend into chaos. Maybe there was a connection. I had witnessed and addresses small scale inefficiency throughout my career, believing that doing so provided a competitive advantage at larger scales. Now all I needed was a name, and the trademarked concept of Micro-Efficiency was born.

Food Poisoning Theory existed in my mind and customer service standards long before writing The Illusion, but moved to the forefront due to the actions and reactions of companies and customers. Food Poisoning Theory emphasizes the last transaction, which by default, becomes the next transaction. The Food Poisoning crux is customers have no loyalty, regardless of rewards and loyalty programs, if the last interaction was poor or the next price is better. All The Illusionist can do is to focus on the customer in front of her and avoid giving customers Food Poisoning in order to encourage future patronage, using tools like Micro-Efficiency and Plus One coverage to ensure the highest possible level of customer service in the moment.

The Theory of Deep Understanding did not exist prior to taking a course on innovation at Grand Canyon University. The Theory of Deep Understanding explained why poor ideas escape executive offices and good ideas from the frontlines are ignored by top executives. The Theory of Deep Understanding states that deep understanding is achieved when a person no longer has to think about a subject. Additionally, people still having to think about the subject will not understand ideas of the person with deep understanding until they reach the same level of understanding. Disconnect occurs when people think they have already reached a level of deep understanding or have stopped trying to reach a level of deep understanding.

The entire premise behind The Illusion of Competence is that middle managers are better qualified than top executives to create, implement, and execute the programs that lead to successful business operations. Like the warmth of a fire, The Illusionist closest to the fire has a stronger appreciation of the heat than The Boss farther from the flames.

The Illusion of Competence, revolutionary in its own right, teaches The Illusionist how to implement and execute innovative programs, embrace existing programs, increase team morale to unprecedented levels, and improve overall sales performance. The Illusion of Competence gets results with executives while putting associates' needs first, a trait beyond the scope of most leadership theories.

The essence of The Illusion of Competence is freedom. The Illusionist gets results, follows corporate policy, and covers The Boss's priorities, leaving her free to create, implement, and execute innovative ideas that are beyond the scope of the company's ability to create on its own. Doing things you know make the business better is very fulfilling, for you, your associates, and at the end of the day, your company.

References:

Balogun, J. (2003). From blaming the middle to harnessing its potential: creating change intermediaries. *British Journal of Management*, 14 (1): 69-84.

Fortune (2016, May 25). *Whole Foods' new, cheaper chain launches today*. Retrieved from http://fortune.com/2016/05/25/whole-foods-new-cheaper-chain-launches-today/

Gandel, S. (2011, August 9). *The 7 habits of highly effective people (1989), by Stephen R. Covey*. Retrieved from http://content.time.com/time/specials/packages/article/0,28804,2086680_2086683_2087685,00.html

Goh, T.N. (2012). Six Sigma at a crossroads. *Current Issues of Business and Law*, 7(1), 17–26

Greenleaf (2016). *What is Servant Leadership*? Retrieved from https://www.greenleaf.org/what-is-servant-leadership/

Guth, W. D., and Macmillan, I.C. (1986). Strategy implementation versus middle management self-interest. *Strategic Management Journal* 7 (4): 313-327.

Hedges, K. (2014, September 23). *If you think leadership development is a waste of time you may be right.* Retrieved fromhttp://www.forbes.com/sites/work-in-progress/2014/09/23/if-you-think-leadership-development-is-a-waste-of-time-you-may-be-right/#3566e56a5dcc

Hrebiniak, L. G. (2008). *Making strategy work. Leading effective execution and change.* (9th ed.). Upper Saddle River: Pearson Education, Inc.

Hsu, T. (2014, February 26). *Data theft at Target hurt sales, earnings during holidays*. Retrieved from http://articles.latimes.com/2014/feb/26/business/l a-fi-target-earnings-hack-20140227

Huy, Q.N. (2012). How middle managers' group-focus emotions and social identities influence strategy implementation. *Strategic Management Journal*, 32(13), 1387-1410.

Kell, J. (2016, July 15). *Why Chipotle's recovery could take years*. Retrieved from http://fortune.com/2016/07/15/chipotle-sales-food-safety/

Kuyvenhoven, R. & Buss, C. W. (2011). A normative view of the role of middle management in the implementation of strategic change. *Journal of Management and Marketing Research*, 8: 1-14

Likert, R. (1961). *New patterns of management*. New York, NY: McGraw-Hill.

Lucas, J. (2015, May 22). *What is the Second Law of Thermodynamics*? Retrieved from http://www.livescience.com/50941-second-law-thermodynamics.html

Malcohm, H. (2014, March 11) *Target sees drop in customer visits after breach*. Retrieved from http://www.usatoday.com/story/money/business/2014/03/11/target-customer-traffic/6262059/

Modern Servant Leader (2016). *Servant Leadership Companies List*. Retrieved from http://modernservantleader.com/featured/servant-leadership-companies-list/

Mojonier, T. (2010, March 18). *Trouble in Toyota City*. Retrieved from http://businesstheory.com/troubles-in-toyota-city-2/

Morrison, M. (2010, January 17). *Deep dive brainstorming technique-IDEO*. Retrieved from https://rapidbi.com/deep-dive-brainstorming-technique-ideo/

Morrison, M. (2010, June 22). *History of SMART objectives*. Retrieved from http://rapidbi.com/history-of-smart-objectives/

Mourdoukoutas, P. (2013, September 27). *A Strategic Mistake That Haunts JC Penney*. Retrieved from http://www.forbes.com/sites/panosmourdoukoutas/2013/09/27/a-strategic-mistake-that-haunts-j-c-penney/#48f765ba3a6c

Psychology Today (2016) *Emotional Intelligence*. Retrieved from

https://www.psychologytoday.com/basics/emotion
al-intelligence

Oyedele, A. (2016, July 28). *Whole Foods shares fall after
sales miss*. Retrieved from
http://www.businessinsider.com/whole-foods-
quarterly-sales-whiff-shares-tank-2016-7

Richardson, K. (2007, January 4). *The 'Six Sigma' factor for
Home Depot*. Retrieved from
http://online.wsj.com/article/SB116787666577566
679.html

Sachs, A. (2011, August 9). *The One Minute Manager
(1982), by Kenneth Blanchard and Spencer Johnson*.
Retrieved from
http://www.time.com/time/specials/packages/artic
le/0,28804,2086680_2086683_2087683,00.html

Sachs, A. (2011, August 9). *Who Moved My Cheese?
(1998), by Spencer Johnson*. Retrieved from

http://www.time.com/time/specials/packages/artic
le/0,28804,2086680_2086683_2087689,00.html

S.M.A.R.T.E.R. Goals (n.d.). Retrieved from

http://www.ucdmc.ucdavis.edu/facultydev/pdfs/S

MARTerGoals.pdf

Spamer, E. (n.d.). *The One Minute Manager: Summary.*

Retrieved from

http://www.bruinleaders.ucla.edu/documents/BLP

_samplebookreview.pdf

Sullivan, M. S. (2015, January 24). *Who said first*

'everything that can be invented has been

invented'? Retrieved from

https://www.quora.com/Who-said-first-everything-

that-can-be-invented-has-been-invented

Sy T, Cˆotˊe S, Saavedra R. (2005). The contagious leader:

impact of the leader's mood on the mood of group

members, group affective tone, and group

processes. *Journal of Applied Psychology 90*: 295–305.

Taneja, S., Pryor, M.G., Sewell, S.M. (2012). Toyota recalls: A strategic leadership perspective. *International Journal of Business & Public Administration 9*: (2) 125-140.

Teresi, D. (2001, July 29). *Ex-colleague charges best-selling author stole his ideas; "One Minute Manager' co-writer says he had a role in "Macgregor' prototype.* Retrieved from http://www.accessmylibrary.com/coms2/summary _0286-784193_ITM

Visionworks (2016). About us. Retrieved from https://www.visionworks.com/about-us

White Dove (n.d.). 7 Habits of Highly Effective People – Summary. Retrieved from

http://www.whitedovebooks.co.uk/7-
habits/summary.htm

Wu, S., Blos, M. F., Wee, H., & Chen, Y. (2010). Can the
Toyota way overcome the recent Toyota setback?
— A study based on the theory of constraints.
Journal of Advanced Manufacturing Systems, *9* (2),
145-146. doi: 10.1142/S0219686710001867

www.ingramcontent.com/pod-product-compliance
Lightning Source LLC
Chambersburg PA
CBHW052318220526
45472CB00001B/175